quick & easy
asian tapas
and noodles

recipes that are easy, delicious and fun

Innovative ideas for entertaining with an Asian flair!
Preparing delicious Asian tapas and noodle dishes is now easier
than ever, thanks to the simple, step-by-step instructions included
in this invaluable book. A quick trip to your local supermarket
for a few basic ingredients is all you need to get started.

PERIPLUS

Contents

MAIL ORDER SOURCES

Finding the ingredients for Asian home cooking has become very simple. Most supermarkets carry staples such as soy sauce, fresh ginger, and fresh lemongrass. Almost every large metropolitan area has Asian markets serving the local population—just check your local business directory. With the Internet, exotic Asian ingredients and cooking utensils can be easily found online. The following list is a good starting point of online merchants offering a wide variety of goods and services.

http://www.asiafoods.com
http://www.geocities.com/MadisonAvenue/8074/VarorE.html
http://dmoz.org/Shopping/Food/Ethnic_and_Regional/Asian/
http://templeofthai.com/
http://www.orientalpantry.com/
http://www.zestyfoods.com/
http://www.thaigrocer.com/Merchant/index.htm
http://asianwok.com/
http://pilipinomart.com/
http://www.indiangrocerynet.com/
http://www.orientalfoodexpress.com/

Noodle and snack dishes have long been a part of Asia's culinary landscape. Stroll down any street in Asia and you'll almost certainly find food stands, restaurants and food courts packed with customers feasting not just on main courses but also on an almost infinite variety of other mouthwatering noodle and snack dishes.

Noodles and snacks are an important part of Asian homestyle cooking also, because these dishes are easy to prepare and fast to cook, and are perfect for a quick meal or for entertaining guests. They give the host a chance to offer hospitality with a range of delicious treats that, while not intended as a full meal, are substantial dishes in their own right, as the collection of noodle and snack recipes in this book will show.

Noodles play a pivotal role as a food in almost every Asian cuisine and each one has its own takes on the noodle theme. Although rice is the mainstay at the Asian table, rice flour, egg or mung bean noodles are just as widespread. Asian cooks have created numerous delectable dishes—from fast stir-fries and healthful salads to invigorating soups and delicate spring rolls or satays.

The noodle recipes in this book are filling, yet easy to prepare, and the sheer variety of dishes on offer mean that you'll be spoilt for choice. Choose from recipes which use a variety of noodles—rice sticks, bean thread and wheat—and are prepared in different ways. Soups, sauces and stir-fries—with an array of main ingredients that include beef, chicken and shrimp to name just a few, offer a delightful array of tastes ranging from sweet to tangy to spicy.

Asian snacks however, are not limited to just noodles, as anyone familiar with Asian food will tell you. The snack recipes in this volume can be served to complement noodle dishes or other main courses. Choose from delicious wraps and rolls, delectable fritters, scrumptious breads and grilled meats with their accompanying dipping sauces.

Whether you're entertaining friends, simply want a quick meal at home or even looking to pack a picnic basket, you can't go wrong with this delicious selection of noodle and snack recipes!

Ingredients Glossary

Asafoetida is a strong-smelling brown tree resin. Known in India as *hing*, it adds an oniony flavor to cooked foods and is believed to aid digestion. Often used in lentil dishes, it is sold in a box or can as a solid lump, or in the form of powder. Use very small amounts—a pinch is enough. Keep well sealed when not in use. If you cannot get it, omit from the recipe.

Black Chinese mushrooms, also known as shiitake

mushrooms, are used widely in Asian cooking. The dried ones must be soaked in hot water to soften before use, from 15 minutes to an hour depending on the thickness. The stems are removed and discarded; only the caps are used. Fresh shiitake mushroom stems can be eaten if the bottoms are trimmed.

Bok choy is a crunchy, leafy green vegetable that is widely used in Chinese cooking. A large vegetable with plump white stalks and dark green leaves, fresh bok choy is available all year round in fresh markets and supermarkets. Substitute choy sum or other leafy greens.

Dried finger-length chilies

Bird's-eye chilies

Fresh finger-length chilies

Dried bird's-eye chilies

Chili peppers come in many shapes, sizes and colors. Fresh Asian **finger-length chilies** are moderately hot. Tiny red, green or orange **bird's-eye chilies** (chili padi) are very hot. **Dried chilies** are usually deseeded, cut into lengths and soaked in warm water to soften before use. **Ground red pepper**, also known as cayenne pepper is made from ground dried chilies. **Chili oil** is made from dried chilies or chili powder infused in oil, and is used to enliven many Sichuan dishes. **Chili paste** consists of ground fresh or dried chilies, sometimes mixed with vinegar and garlic and sold in jars. **Sichuan chili paste** is made from dried chilies, soaked and ground with a touch of oil. **Chili sauce** is made by mixing ground chilies with water and seasoning the mixture with

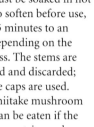

Thai basil
(horapa)

Lemon basil
(manglak)

Basil is used as a seasoning and garnish in many Asian cuisines. Two varieties are used in this book. **Thai basil** (*horapa*) tastes rather like Italian sweet basil but with an added hint of anise, and is used in red and green curries as well as salads and stir-fries. It is available year round. If you cannot find it, use Italian basil. **Lemon basil** (*manglak*) has a lemony flavor that goes well with soups and salads. Basil doesn't store well, so buy it just before you intend to use it.

salt, sugar and vinegar or lime juice. It is available bottled and in jars.

Chinese celery has much smaller and thinner stems than the normal Western variety, and has a very intense, parsley-like flavor. The leaves and sometimes the stems are added to soups, rice dishes and stir-fried vegetables. This type of celery is obtainable in Asian specialty stores—use celery leaves or Italian parsley as a substitute.

Choy sum or **chye sim**, also known as Chinese flowering cabbage, is a leafy green vegetable with crisp crunchy stems. Available in supermarkets in Asia, it is now increasingly available in Western countries too. Substitute bok choy or any other leafy green vegetable.

Coconut milk is obtain by squeezing the flesh of freshly grated coconuts. To obtain **thick coconut milk**, add 1 cup (250 ml) of water to the grated flesh of one coconut, then squeeze and strain. Although freshly squeezed milk has more flavor, it is far more convenient to use the canned or packet variety. **Grated fresh coconut** can be purchased from Asian markets or you can grate it yourself. Purchase coconuts that are heavy and have a lot of juice in them. Crack the coconut open and drain the juice. Break the shell into smaller pieces by turning it on a firm surface and knocking it with a mallet. Use a knife to release the meat from the shell. Remove the flesh from the shell and peel the brown outer skin using a vegetable peeler. Grate the flesh in a blender or food processor, adding a bit of water to help the blades turn.

Coriander is an indispensable herb and spice in Asian cooking. **Coriander seeds** are roasted and then ground in spice pastes. **Coriander roots** are used in the same way, while **coriander leaves** (also known as cilantro or Chinese parsley) are used as a herb and a garnish.

Cumin seeds (*jeera*) are pale brown in color and usually partnered with coriander seeds in basic spice mixes. They impart an intense, earthy flavor to foods and are often dry-roasted or flash-cooked in oil to intensify their flavor.

Curry leaves come in sprigs of 8–15, dark green leaves and are used to flavor Indian curries. Fresh curry leaves should be used within a few days of purchase. Dried curry leaves keep well if stored in a dry place but do not have as much flavor. There is no good substitute. Curry leaves are available in Indian food stores and internet grocers.

Channa Dal

Urad dal or blackgram dal

Dal refers to a wide variety of split peas and beans. **Channa dal** or **Bengal gram** resembles a yellow split pea but is smaller. **Channa flour** is made by milling channa dal. It is very fine in texture and pale yellow in color. Finely ground chickpea flour may be used as a substitute. **Urad dal** or **blackgram dal** is sold either with its black skin on or husked, when it is creamy white in color.

Dried shrimp are sold in plastic packets or in bins in Asian markets. Choose dried shrimp that are pink in color and soak them in water to soften before use.

Fish sauce is made from salted, fermented fish or shrimp. Good quality fish sauce is golden-brown in color and has a salty tang. It is available in bottles in most supermarkets.

Galangal is similar in appearance to ginger and a member of the same family. This aromatic root has a distinctive flavor that is used in dishes throughout Asia. Dried galangal lacks the fragrance of fresh galangal, so try to buy it fresh. It can be sliced and kept sealed in the freezer for several months.

Garam masala is an Indian blend of ground spices, usually including cinnamon, cardamon, cloves, fennel and black pepper. Pre-blended garam masala can be bought from any store specializing in spices. Store in an airtight jar away from heat or sunlight.

Ghee is the rich, delicious clarified butter oil used as the main oil in Indian cooking. It is made by removing the milk solids from butter, and is therefore known as "clarified butter oil." It keeps well at room temperature. Substitute vegetable oil or butter.

Glutinous rice is a variety of rice that becomes very sticky when cooked. Mainly used in snacks, sweets and desserts, it is available in packets in any Asian food store.

Ground red pepper is a pungent red powder made from ground dried chili peppers, also known as cayenne pepper. Substitute dried red chili flakes.

Hoisin sauce consists of fermented soybeans, garlic, chilies, and vinegar. The sauce is thick and dark and has a sweet, salty flavor. Commercially bottled or canned hoisin sauce is available in most grocery stores.

Kaffir lime is also known as fragrant lime. This citrus fruit has an intensely fragrant skin but virtually no juice. The grated skin or rind is used as a seasoning. **Kaffir lime leaves** are the fragrant leaves of the kaffir lime plant, which are used whole in soups and curries, or shredded finely and added to salads.

Nutmegs are the seeds of the nutmeg tree, covered with a lacy membrane called **mace**. Buy whole nutmegs and grate them as needed since ground nutmeg quickly looses its flavor. Use nutmeg powder if you cannot get whole nutmegs.

Oyster sauce is a thick sauce made from ground oysters, water, salt, cornstarch and caramel coloring. It is often used in Chinese cooking to intensify the flavor of the food. It is often splashed onto stir-fried vegetables and meat dishes, and sometimes added to marinades. Oyster sauce should be refrigerated after opening. Vegetarians should look for the version sold as "mushroom oyster sauce".

Palm sugar is made from the sap of various palm fruits. Palm sugar varies in color from gold to dark brown. It is less sweet than cane sugar and has a distinct, rich flavor. Dark brown sugar, maple syrup or a mixture of sugar and molasses are good substitutes.

Plum sauce is a sweet Chinese sauce made from plums, vinegar and sugar.

Fresh yellow wheat noodles

Dried rice vermicelli

Rice stick noodles

Noodles are a universal favorite in Asia. Both fresh and dried noodles are made from either wheat, rice or mung bean flour. **Fresh yellow wheat noodles** are thick, spaghetti-like noodles made from wheat flour and egg. Substitute fresh spaghetti or fettucini if you cannot find them. **Dried rice vermicelli** are very fine rice threads that must be plunged into hot water to soften before use. **Rice stick noodles** (also known as "river noodles", *kway teow* or *hofun*) are wide, flat rice noodles sold fresh in Asian markets. If not available, use dried rice stick noodles instead.

Sold in jars in Asian grocery stores and well stocked supermarkets, plum sauce should be refrigerated after opening.

Sesame seeds are small and pear-shaped and come in several colors—white, yellow, brown or black—though all are white on the inside when hulled.

Sesame oil is extracted from sesame seeds that have been toasted, producing a dark, dense and highly aromatic oil that is used for marinades, sauces and soups, or as a table condiment. Its nutty, smokey flavor has become a hallmark of Chinese cuisine.

Sesame paste is made from ground, roasted sesame seeds and comes in glass jars covered with oil. It is quite hard and needs to be mixed with a little sesame oil or water to make it into a smooth paste. If you can't find it, use Middle Eastern tahini mixed with some sesame oil to give it more flavor. Not to be confused with sweet sesame paste made from black sesame

Dark soy sauce   Light soy sauce   Sweet black sauce

Soy sauce is a fermented sauce brewed from soybeans, water, wheat and salt. **Regular** or **light soy sauce** is very salty and used as a table dip and cooking seasoning. **Dark soy sauce** is denser and less salty and adds a smoky flavor to dishes. **Sweet black soy sauce** is a thick, fragrant sauce used in marinades and sauces.

seeds which is used in some snacks and desserts.

Shallots are small, round onions with thin red skins that add a sweet oniony flavor to countless dishes. They are added to spice pastes or sliced, deep-fried and used as garnish.

Shrimp paste, comes in two forms, dried and wet. Dried shrimp paste, also known as *belachan,* is a dense mixture of fermented ground shrimp that must be toasted before use—either wrapped in foil and dry-roasted or

toasted over a gas flame on the tip of a metal skewer or back of a spoon. **Wet shrimp paste** is also known as *hae ko* or *petis.* This thick black paste has a strong fishy flavor. It is sold in jars and may be added to recipes straight from the jar.

Sichuan peppercorns, also known as Chinese pepper or flower pepper (*hua jiao*), have a sharp pungency that tingles and slightly numbs the lips and tongue—an effect known in Chinese as *ma la* "numb hot".

Spring roll wrappers are thin sheets of light, pliable pastry made from wheat flour, eggs and salt. These wrappers are used to wrap a variety of fillings, then deep-fried until golden brown. They are available both fresh and frozen in well-stocked supermarkets and Asian markets. They are also sold in the West as egg roll wrappers, and are often called skins, rather than wrappers in Asia. Indonesian or Filipino lumpia skins are good substitutes.

Tamarind is the fruit of the tamarind tree—which is enclosed by a long seed pod. The dried pulp is sold in packets or jars and generally still has some seeds and pod fibers mixed in. It is used as a souring agent in many dishes. To obtain **tamarind juice**, soak the pulp in warm water for 5 minutes, mash well and then strain and discard the seeds and fibers.

Water chestnuts are small, acorn-shaped roots with a brown leathery skin on the outside and a crisp, juicy-sweet flesh inside. The dark brown skin should be peeled before eating, and it is well worth using fresh water chestnuts if you can find them. Their crisp texture and sweet flavor make them popular in salads, stir-fried vegetable dishes and desserts. Canned water chestnuts are also widely available.

Condiments, Sauces and Dips

The following dips, pastes, sauces and side dishes are either recipes in their own right or basic components of other recipes featured later in this book.

Sweet and Sour Plum or Apricot Sauce

$^1/_2$ cup (125 ml) water
1 cup (7 oz/200 g) sugar
$^1/_2$ cup (125 ml) vinegar
1 red finger-length chili, finely chopped (optional)
3 cloves garlic, peeled and finely chopped
2 tablespoons Chinese plum sauce or Japanese apricot sauce (apricot or plum jam or marmalade may also be used)

1 Combine the water, sugar and vinegar in a small saucepan. Bring to a boil over high heat, then reduce the heat to low. Cook until the mixture begins to thicken, about 40 minutes.
2 Add the red chili, garlic and apricot or plum sauce. Stir a few times. Remove from the heat and cool before serving.

Red Curry Paste

1 tablespoon coriander seeds
1 teaspoon cumin seeds
5 dried red chilies, deseeded and soaked in hot water for 15 minutes
3 tablespoons sliced shallots
8 cloves garlic, smashed
2-3 thin slices galangal
2 tablespoons sliced lemongrass, tender inner part of bottom third only
2 teaspoons grated kaffir lime rind
1 tablespoon chopped coriander (cilantro) roots
10 black peppercorns
1 teaspoon dried shrimp paste (*belachan*), roasted

Dry-fry the coriander and cumin seeds in a skillet over low heat for about 5 minutes, then grind to a powder in a blender. Add the remaining ingredients, except the shrimp paste, and grind well. Add the shrimp paste and grind again to obtain about $3/4$ cup (180 ml) of fine-textured curry paste.

Cucumber Salad

2 tablespoons sugar
1 teaspoon salt
$1/3$ cup (90 ml) warm water
2 tablespoons vinegar
3 shallots, thinly sliced
1 red finger-length chili, deseeded and sliced
1 cucumber, peeled, quartered lengthwise and thinly sliced

1 Dissolve the sugar and salt in the water. Add the vinegar.
2 Place the shallots and the chili slices on top of the cucumber in a serving bowl. Pour the sugar water mixture over the top.

Vietnamese Fish Sauce Dip

2 to 3 red finger-length chilies, deseeded and sliced
3 cloves garlic
$1/4$ cup (2 oz/50 g) sugar
3 tablespoons freshly-squeezed lime juice
1 tablespoon vinegar
3 tablespoons fish sauce
$1/2$ cup (125 ml) water
$1/2$ teaspoon salt

Yields 1 cup (250 ml)
Preparation time: **10 mins**

Grind the chilies and garlic to a coarse paste in a mortar or blender, then combine with all the other ingredients and mix until the sugar is dissolved.

Sweet and Spicy Peanut Sauce

$1/4$ cup (60 ml) water
$1/2$ cup (4 oz/100 g) sugar
1 teaspoon salt
$1/4$ cup (60 ml) vinegar
$1/2$ teaspoon minced
  fresh red chili
$1/4$ cup (2 oz/45 g)
  roasted peanuts, ground

1 Bring the water, sugar and salt to a boil in a saucepan.
2 Reduce the heat to low and simmer for about 15 minutes.
3 Remove from the heat. Stir in the vinegar and minced chili. Let it cool and add the peanuts before serving.

Spicy-sweet Thai Dip

$1/4$ cup (1 oz/30 g)
  onions, thinly sliced
1 tablespoon sliced
  lemongrass, tender inner
  part of bottom third only
1 tablespoon fresh
  ginger, grated
$1/2$ tablespoon dried
  shrimp paste (*belachan*)
1 cup (4 oz/100 g)
  grated fresh coconut
$1/4$ cup (1 oz/30 g) dried
  shrimp
$1 1/2$ teaspoons salt
2 cups (500 ml) plus
  $1/2$ to $3/4$ cups
  (125 to 185 ml) water
$1 1/4$ cups (8 oz/250 g)
  palm sugar
Crushed peanuts for
  garnish

1 Roast the onions, lemongrass, ginger and dried shrimp paste on a flat baking sheet in the oven at 250°F (120°C) until golden, about 15 minutes. Roast the coconut at 350°F (180°C) until golden brown, stirring often, about 10 minutes.
2 Put the onions, lemongrass, ginger, dried shrimp paste, coconut, dried shrimp and salt into a blender and add $1/2$ cup (125 ml) water gradually and process, adding more water if necessary. Process for a few seconds; the consistency does not need to be smooth.
3 Transfer the mixture to a large saucepan and add 2 cups (500 ml) water and the palm sugar. Bring the mixture to a boil over medium heat, then reduce the heat to medium–low and cook for 1 hour and 15 minutes, stirring occasionally. Remove from the heat and cool.

Preparation time: **15 mins**
Cooking time: **1 hour 45 mins**

Shrimp Paste Dip *(Hae Ko)*

2 tablespoons shrimp
  paste (*hae ko* or *petis*)
2 tablespoons hot water

Combine the shrimp paste and water and serve in small dipping bowls, one per person.

Chicken Stock

12 cups (3 liters) water
1 fresh chicken (about
  3 lbs/1$^1/_2$ kgs)
1 tablespoon white pep-
  percorns
1 cup (150 g) sliced onions
1 medium carrot, sliced
1 stalk Chinese celery,
  sliced

$^1/_4$ teaspoon salt
$^1/_4$ teaspoon ground
  white pepper

Makes 1$^1/_2$ liters (6 cups)
Preparation time: **10 mins**
Cooking time: **2 hours**

Bring all the ingredients to a boil in a stockpot.
Reduce the heat to low and simmer for 2 to 3 hours,
skimming off the foam and fat that float to the surface, until the stock is reduced to half. Remove from
the heat, strain the stock and set aside to cool.

Vietnamese Peanut Sauce

$^3/_4$ cup (185 ml) water
$^1/_4$ cup (60 ml) hoisin
  sauce
1 teaspoon tamarind
  pulp soaked in 1 table-
  spoon warm water,
  mashed and strained to
  obtain the juice

$^1/_2$ cup (4 oz/120 g)
  crunchy peanut butter

Makes 1$^1/_2$ cup (375 ml)
Preparation time: **5 mins**
Cooking time: **10 mins**

Combine all the ingredients in a bowl and mix until
well blended.

Vietnamese Caramel Sauce

$^2/_3$ cup (4$^1/_2$ oz/135 g)
  sugar
$^1/_2$ cup (125 ml) fish
  sauce
8 shallots, thinly sliced
$^1/_2$ teaspoon freshly
  ground black pepper

Makes $^2/_3$ cup (135 ml)
Preparation time: **5 mins**
Cooking time: **10 mins**

Heat the sugar over low heat in a skillet, stirring
constantly, until it begins to melt and caramelize,
3 to 5 minutes. Remove from the heat and add the fish
sauce. Return the pan to the heat and bring the mixture
to a boil over medium heat. Simmer uncovered for
3 to 5 minutes, stirring constantly until the mixture
turns into a thick syrup. Add the shallots and ground
black pepper, mix well and remove from the heat.

Sweet-sour Chili Dip

4 fresh red or green fin-
  ger-length chilies, sliced
2 tablespoons vinegar
Sugar to taste

Combine the chili and vinegar in a small bowl, then add sugar to taste.

Crispy Fried Garlic or Shallots

Peeled garlic cloves or
  shallots
Oil, for frying

1 Slice the garlic or shallots lengthwise. Take care to ensure that all slices are of an even thickness, or they will not cook evenly.
2 Heat the oil in a saucepan until just smoking, add the garlic or shallots and stir-fry over low heat for 1 to 2 minutes, stirring constantly, until golden brown and crispy. Remove with a slotted spoon and drain on paper towels. When cool, store in an air-tight container.

Green Onion (Scallion) Oil or Garlic Oil

$1/4$ cup (60 ml) oil
2 green onions (scallions),
  thinly sliced or 2 tablespoons garlic, minced

Heat the oil over medium heat in a small saucepan. Remove the saucepan from the heat and add the green onions or garlic. Let the mixture cool to room temperature and store in a tightly sealed jar where it will stay fresh for up to one week.

Roasted Rice Powder

$1/2$ cup (4 oz/120 g)
  uncooked long-grain or
  glutinous rice

Spread the uncooked long-grain or glutinous rice grains on a baking sheet and bake, stirring often, in a 500°F (250°C) oven until the rice turns brown. Alternatively, spread the rice grains out in an oil-free skillet and cook over medium–low heat, stirring often, until it browns and becomes fragrant. Remove the rice grains from the heat and grind in a blender until the grains resemble crushed black peppercorns. Stores well in a tightly sealed container for several months.

Sweet Lime Chutney

1 lb (500 g) limes, deseeded and finely chopped
2 tablespoons salt
2 onions, chopped (about 1¹/₂ cups)
2 tablespoons mustard seeds, roasted and coarsely ground
1¹/₂ cups (10 oz/300 g) sugar
1¹/₄ cups (300 ml) white vinegar

2 teaspoons ground red pepper
1 teaspoon ground turmeric
Scant ³/₄ cup (4 oz/100 g) raisins

Serves 6
Preparation time: 15 mins
Cooking time: 1 hour 15 mins

Place the chopped lime pieces in a stainless steel saucepan. Sprinkle with the salt and mix well. Add all the remaining ingredients and simmer over low heat until the lime pieces become tender and the chutney thickens, about 1 hour 15 minutes. Serve as an accompaniment.

Sweet Tomato Date Chutney

2 tablespoons oil
¹/₂ teaspoon urad dal
¹/₂ teaspoon mustard seeds
¹/₂ teaspoon cumin seeds
¹/₂ teaspoon fennel seeds
1 bay leaf
¹/₄ cup (2¹/₂ oz/75 g) tamarind pulp mixed with 50 ml (¹/₄ cup) water, mashed and strained to obtain the juice
2³/₄ cups (1 lb/500 g) diced fresh tomatoes, or canned whole tomatoes
1 cup (7 oz/200 g) sugar
1 red finger-length chilli, finely sliced
1 cup (4 oz/125 g) pitted dates, quartered
³/₄ teaspoon salt

1 Heat the oil in a wok or skillet over low heat and stir-fry the dal and spices and the bay leaf until aromatic, 4 to 5 minutes.
2 Add the remaining ingredients, bring to a boil, then lower the heat and simmer until the chutney thickens, about 45 minutes. Allow to cool, then store in a sealed container in the refrigerator.

Fennel seeds look like cumin seeds but are larger and paler. They add a sweet fragrance to Indian dishes, with a flavour similar to liquorice or anise. The seeds are used whole or ground.

Serves 6
Preparation time: 10 mins
Cooking time: 45 mins

Spicy Mango Coconut Chutney

1¼ cups (7 oz/200 g) peeled and diced unripe mango
2½ cups (250 g) grated fresh coconut
4 green finger-length chilies, cut into lengths
½ teaspoon salt
1½ tablespoons oil
½ teaspoon urad dal
½ teaspoon mustard seeds
1 sprig curry leaves
¼ teaspoon asafoetida

1 Coarsely grind the diced mango, coconut, green chilies and salt in a blender and set aside.
2 In a small saucepan, heat the oil and fry the urad dal over low heat until golden brown. Add the mustard seeds and curry leaves and fry until the seeds pop. Add the asafoetida, mix well and turn off the heat.
3 Add the fried spices to the ground ingredients and mix well. Serve as an accompaniment to rice or breads.

Serves 6
Preparation time: 10 mins
Cooking time: 10 mins

Coriander Coconut Chutney

2 cups (4 oz/100 g) fresh coriander leaves (cilantro), chopped
5 cups (500 g) grated fresh coconut
4 green finger-length chilies, sliced into lengths
4 tablespoons freshly-squeezed lime juice
3 slices ginger
1 teaspoon salt
½ cup (125 ml) water

Place all the ingredients in a food processor or blender and process until smooth. Serve with thosai, idli or any savory snacks.

Serves 6
Preparation time: 20 mins

Four types of Indian chutney in a typical serving tray.

Fresh Chinese Spring Rolls

2 sweet dried Chinese sausages (*lap cheong*, see note)
1 tablespoon oil
2 eggs, lightly beaten
8 spring roll wrappers
1 small cucumber, peeled and cut into strips
3 cakes (10 oz/300 g each) firm tofu, cut into cubes (page 47)
8 green onions (scallions), trimmed
1 cup (4 oz/120 g) cooked crabmeat, leave some to garnish

8 oz (250 g) bean sprouts, tails removed, blanched for 2 minutes

Sauce
1 cup (250 ml) Chicken Stock (page 12) or water
1/4 cup (2 oz/50 g) palm sugar
2 tablespoons tamarind pulp soaked in 1/4 cup (60 ml) water, mashed and strained to obtain the juice
1/2 cup (3 oz/90 g) roasted peanuts, finely ground

2 tablespoons Crispy Fried Shallots (page 13)
1 tablespoon fish sauce
1 tablespoon sweet black soy sauce (see note)
1 tablespoon oyster sauce
1 teaspoon salt
4 teaspoons tapioca flour or cornstarch mixed with 1/4 cup (60 ml) water
1/4 teaspoon five spice powder (page 80)
1/4 cup (1 oz/30 g) dry-roasted sesame seeds

1 Steam the Chinese sausages for 5 to 6 minutes, cool and then cut them into 8 thin strips lengthwise.
2 Heat the oil in a wok or skillet over medium heat and fry the eggs into an omelet. Cut the omelet into 8 long pieces and set aside.
3 Place a spring roll wrapper on a flat surface and put a piece of sausage, omelet, cucumber, tofu, green onion, 2 tablespoons of crabmeat and some bean sprouts on the wrapper. Roll the wrapper up tightly. Repeat until you use all the wrappers.
4 To make the Sauce, combine all the ingredients, except the sesame seeds, in a saucepan. Cook over medium heat until the mixture boils, stir a few times. Add the sesame seeds when the mixture begins to thicken. Transfer to a serving dish.
5 Serve the rolls as they are, or steam the rolls for 1 to 2 minutes in a steamer or microwave oven. Garnish each roll with some crabmeat and serve with the Sauce on the side or drizzle over the top.

Sweet dried Chinese sausages (*lap cheong*) are perfumed with rose-flavored wine. Generally sold in pairs, these sausages keep without refrigeration and are normally sliced and cooked with other ingredients rather than being eaten on their own. They should not be eaten raw. Substitute any sweet, dried sausage or meat jerky.

Sweet black soy sauce is not widely available in the West but can be approximated by adding 1/2 teaspoon brown sugar to 1 tablespoon of dark soy sauce. Hoisin sauce mixed with soy sauce also makes a good substitute.

Serves 8
Preparation time: 20 mins
Assembling time: 20 mins

Fold the closest end of the wrapper over the filling, then fold in the sides and roll up once

Place two halves of a shrimp on the roll and continue to roll the wrapper up tightly.

Vietnamese Shrimp and Pork Salad Rolls

These rolls are like Vietnamese salad wrapped in rice paper wrappers. The aromatic herbs in the rolls lend a refreshing taste. If you are looking for a unique summer picnic dish, these are perfect!

2 cups (500 ml) water
1 green onion (scallion)
8 oz (250 g) lean pork
10 oz (300 g) fresh
  medium shrimp
12 sheets rice paper
  wrappers (see note)
1 small head butter lettuce, leaves washed
  and separated
1 4-oz (100-g) packet
  dried rice vermicelli
  (*beehoon or mifen*),
  blanched for 1 to 2
  minutes until soft, then
  rinsed with cold water
  and drained
1 baby cucumber, quartered and thinly sliced
1 small carrot, grated
1 bunch fresh coriander
  leaves (cilantro), sliced
1 portion Vietnamese
  Peanut Sauce (page 12)

Makes 12 rolls
Preparation time: 30 mins
Cooking time: 25 mins

1 Bring the water and green onion to a boil over medium heat in a saucepan and poach the pork for 7 to 10 minutes until cooked. Remove and set aside to cool. Slice the pork into thin strips.

2 Bring the same pot of water to a boil again and poach the shrimp for 1 to 2 minutes until pink or just cooked. Remove and plunge into cold water to cool. Peel, devein and halve each shrimp lengthwise. Set aside.

3 To make a spring roll, briefly dip a rice paper wrapper in a bowl of water until soft. Remove and place on a dry surface, smoothing it with your fingers. Place a lettuce leaf onto the wrapper, closer to one edge, and top with some pork strips, rice vermicelli, cucumber and carrot. Fold the closest edge of the wrapper over the filling, then fold in the sides and roll up halfway. Place 2 halves of a shrimp, side by side, along the roll and top with the coriander leaves, then continue to roll up tightly to complete the folding. Repeat until all the ingredients are used up.

4 Arrange the spring rolls on a serving platter and serve with serving bowls of Vietnamese Peanut Sauce on the side.

Vietnamese rice paper wrappers are sold dried in plastic packets of 10 or 20. Other types of spring roll or wonton wrappers may substitute for rice paper wrappers although most of them are made from wheat flour and eggs, and the taste is therefore quite different.

Crispy Thai Spring Rolls

1 lb (500 g) ground pork
or chicken
4 oz (100 g) dried bean
thread noodles (see
note)
2 dried black Chinese
mushrooms, soaked in
warm water for 20 min-
utes, stems discarded
and caps sliced
3 cups (7 oz/200 g)
green cabbage, shredded
2 cups (4 oz/100 g) bean
sprouts, tails removed,
blanched and roughly
chopped
1 carrot, grated
2 cloves garlic, finely
chopped
2 tablespoons fresh
coriander leaves
(cilantro), chopped
2 tablespoons fish sauce
1 tablespoon soy sauce
1 teaspoon salt
1 teaspoon ground white
pepper
1 large egg
24 spring roll wrappers
1 tablespoon cornstarch
mixed with enough
water to form paste
3 cups (750 ml) oil, for
deep-frying
1 cup (250 ml) Sweet
and Spicy Peanut Sauce
(page 11)

1 Soak the dried bean thread noodles in water for 30 minutes, drain in a colander and cut into lengths.

2 Combine all the ingredients except the wrappers, cornstarch paste and oil in a mixing bowl. Lay a spring roll wrapper on a flat surface and place 2 table-spoons of the filling on the lower half of the wrapper. Fold the bottom edge of the wrapper over the filling. Next, fold the right and left edges over the first fold, then roll tightly. Seal the edge of roll with the corn-starch paste. Repeat until the wrappers and filling are finished.

3 Heat the oil in a wok over high heat. Place the rolls, a few at a time, into the oil and deep-fry until golden brown. Remove with a slotted spoon or tongs. Drain on paper towels. Serve hot with the Sweet and Spicy Peanut Sauce.

Bean thread noodles, also known as "cellophane" or "glass" noodles, are thin, clear strands made from mung bean starch and water. Soak in hot water for 15 minutes to soften. Available from Asian food stores.

Makes 24 rolls
Preparation time: 30 min + 30 mins soaking
Cooking time: 20 mins

Thai-style Egg Salad

12 leaves leafy green lettuce
6 hard-boiled eggs, shelled and thinly sliced
2 small shallots, thinly sliced
$^1/_2$ cup (1 oz/30 g) Chinese celery or Italian parsley, chopped
$^1/_4$ cup (2 oz/50 g) Crispy Fried Shallots (page 13)
2 tablespoons Crispy Fried Garlic (page 13)
1 sprig fresh coriander leaves (cilantro), coarsely chopped

Dressing
1 tablespoons Thai chili paste (*nam prik pao,* see note)
2 tablespoons soy sauce
2 tablespoons freshly-squeezed lime juice
1 teaspoons sugar

1 Line a serving platter with the lettuce leaves. Place the egg slices on the leaves and sprinkle with the shallots, Chinese celery,Crispy Fried Garlic and Shallots, and fresh coriander leaves.
2 Combine the Dressing ingredients and pour over the salad just before serving.

Thai chili paste (*nam prik pao*) is a rich chili paste made from chilies, shallots, garlic, sugar, dried shrimp, fish sauce and sometimes tamarind. It is used as a spicy dip or added to soups and noodles. Chili paste comes in different strengths and is available in jars or plastic tubs in specialty stores.

Serves 4–6
Preparation time: **20 mins**
Cooking time: **5 mins**

Vietnamese Pork and Shrimp Crêpes

1 cup (4 oz/125 g) rice flour
1 cup (250 ml) water
1 cup (250 ml) thick coconut milk
$1/2$ teaspoon salt
$1/4$ teaspoon ground turmeric
1 to 2 tablespoons oil
3 cups (5 oz/150 g) bean sprouts, tails removed
2 green onions (scallions), minced
6 fresh black Chinese mushrooms, soaked in warm water for 20 minutes, stems discarded and caps sliced
1 portion Vietnamese Fish Sauce Dip (page 10)

Filling
7 oz (200 g) pork, very thinly sliced
8 oz (250 g) fresh medium shrimp, peeled and deveined
4 cloves garlic, minced
1 tablespoon fish sauce
$1/2$ teaspoon sugar
2 tablespoons oil
1 onion, halved and sliced

Lettuce Wraps
20 butter lettuce leaves, rinsed and trimmed
Sprigs of mint leaves
Sprigs of fresh coriander leaves (cilantro)
1 cucumber, peeled and thinly sliced

1 Make the Filling by combining the pork, shrimp, garlic, fish sauce and sugar in a large bowl and mixing well. Heat the oil in a wok or skillet over medium heat and stir-fry the onion slices for 1 to 2 minutes until fragrant and translucent. Add the pork and shrimp mixture, and stir-fry until the shrimp turn pink, 2 to 3 minutes. Remove and set aside.

2 To make the crêpe, mix the rice flour, water, coconut milk, salt and turmeric in a mixing bowl until a smooth batter is obtained. Set aside for 10 minutes, then strain to remove any lumps.

3 Heat a little oil in a non-stick skillet over medium heat, turning to grease the sides. When the pan is hot, pour in $1/3$ cup (85 ml) of the batter and turn the pan to obtain a thin round layer of batter, about 8 in (20 cm) in diameter. Scatter a handful of the bean sprouts, green onions and mushroom onto the crêpe, followed by 2 heaping tablespoons of the Filling on one half of the crêpe. Reduce the heat to low, cover the pan and continue to fry for 3 to 4 minutes, until the crêpe turns golden brown and crispy. Fold the crêpe in half and slide it onto a plate. Repeat until all the batter and Filling are used up.

4 Slice the crêpe into sections and arrange with the Lettuce Wraps on a large serving platter. Serve immediately with a bowl of Vietnamese Fish Sauce Dip on the side.

5. To serve, wrap each section of the crêpe in a lettuce leaf together with some mint, coriander leaves and cucumber, and dip in the Vietnamese Fish Sauce Dip.

Makes 5 to 6 crêpês or serves 4 to 6
Preparation time: **30 mins**
Cooking time: **40 mins**

Thai Lettuce Leaf Cups

The trick to enjoying this traditional Thai snack is in sampling a bit of everything in the leaf cup—the combined flavors and textures make this a real treat. Serve with Spicy-sweet Thai Dip.

1 lime or lemon, peeled and finely diced
2 in (5 cm) fresh ginger, peeled and diced
1 shallot, peeled and diced
$^1/_4$ cup (1 oz/30 g) tiny dried shrimp or meat jerky or salami or sweet dried Chinese sausages (*lap cheong*), finely diced (see note)
1 tablespoon thinly sliced fresh red finger-length chilies
$^1/_4$ cup (2 oz/45 g) roasted unsalted peanuts, skins removed
$^1/_4$ cup (1$^1/_3$ oz/40 g) dry-roasted grated coconut (see note)
10 small leaves leafy green lettuce or *bok choy* leaves
1 cup (250 ml) Spicy-sweet Thai Dip (page 11)

1 Arrange the leaf cup ingredients in separate piles on a serving tray. Add the crushed peanuts to the Spicy-sweet Thai Dip and serve in a small dish.
2 To serve, make a triangular cone from a leaf and fill the cone with 1 teaspoon coconut. Add 1 piece of each of the other ingredients. Spoon $^1/_2$ teaspoon Spicy-sweet Thai Dip over the contents and fold the leaf over to cover the filling before eating.

Sweet dried Chinese sausages (*lap cheong*) are perfumed with rose-flavored wine. Generally sold in pairs, these sausages keep without refrigeration and are normally sliced and cooked with other ingredients rather than being eaten on their own. They should not be eaten raw. Substitute any sweet, dried sausage or meat jerky.

Heat a wok over very low heat, add the **grated coconut** and fry over very low heat, tossing them continually, until fragrant and golden brown, about 10 minutes. Set aside to cool before using.

Serves 12
Preparation and cooking time: **2 hours**

Tapioca Dumplings with Pork Filling

2 cups (10 oz/300 g) dried tapioca pearls or tapioca flour (see note)
1 cup (250 ml) warm water
4 tablespoons Garlic Oil (page 13)
10 cups (2$^1/_2$ liters) water
2 tablespoons Crispy Fried Garlic (page 13), as garnish
1 head leafy green lettuce, leaves separated and rinsed
9 sprigs fresh coriander leaves (cilantro)

Filling
$^1/_4$ cup (1 oz/30 g) diced preserved salted radish (see note)
3 fresh coriander (cilantro) roots
4 cloves garlic, peeled
$^1/_2$ teaspoon whole black peppercorns
2 tablespoons oil
1 cup (7 oz/200 g) ground pork
1 cup (5 oz/150 g) diced shallots or onions
$^1/_2$ cup (4 oz/100 g) palm sugar
$^1/_4$ cup (60 ml) fish sauce
$^2/_3$ cup (3 oz/90 g) ground roasted peanuts

Makes 60
Preparation time: **50 mins**
Cooking time: **20 mins**

1 Combine the tapioca pearls or flour and warm water in a mixing bowl and stir with a wooden spoon until mixed. Knead into a soft dough. Cover with a moist cloth and set aside.
2 To make the Filling, wash the salted radish, squeeze dry and set aside. Using a pestle and mortar, pound the coriander roots, garlic and peppercorns until fine.
3 Heat the 2 tablespoons of oil over medium heat in a wok. Cook the pounded mixture until fragrant, about 3 minutes. Add the pork and keep stirring, breaking up any lumps. Add the onion and salted radish. Stir in the palm sugar and fish sauce and continue to cook until the liquid is almost evaporated. Add the peanuts. Stir until the Filling mixture thickens. Remove from the heat and cool.
4 To make the dumplings, dip your hands in cold water. Take about 1 teaspoon of the tapioca dough and shape it into a small ball, then flatten it. Place 1 teaspoon of the Filling in the center and gather the edges up to form a dumpling. Repeat until all the remaining dough and Filling are used up.
5 Use the Garlic Oil to oil a serving platter. Bring the 10 cups (2$^1/_2$ liters) of water to a boil in a large saucepan. Drop the tapioca dumplings into the water, about 10 pieces at a time. When they float to the surface, use a slotted spoon to scoop them out, place them on the serving platter and sprinkle with the Crispy Fried Garlic. Alternatively, steam the dumplings over high heat for 5 minutes. Serve with the lettuce leaves and coriander leaves for wrapping.

Preserved salted radish or chai poh is pickled Japanese radish or daikon. Often added to dishes for its crunchy texture and salty flavor, it is available at Asian markets.

Tapioca pearls are tiny beads made from cassava starch. The uncooked pearls are hard and white when dried, but turn soft and translucent when cooked. Tapioca pearls are often used in desserts and to thicken dough. The pearls are sold in plastic packets in Asian markets.

Steamed Shrimp Wonton Dumplings

30 circular wonton wrappers (see note)

3 tablespoons Garlic Oil (page 13)

$1/4$ cup (60 ml) Sweet-sour Chili Dip (page 13)

$1^1/4$ in (3 cm) fresh ginger, very finely sliced

Filling

3 cloves garlic

3 fresh coriander (cilantro) roots

10 whole black peppercorns

1 cup (7 oz/200 g) ground pork

5 oz (150 g) fresh shrimp, chopped

1 small onion, chopped

6 water chestnuts, peeled and diced

1 tablespoon cornstarch

1 tablespoon sugar

1 teaspoon fish sauce

1 teaspoon soy sauce

$1/2$ teaspoon salt

1 To make the Filling, grind the garlic, coriander roots and peppercorns until fine. Combine this paste with the rest of the Filling ingredients in a mixing bowl until well blended.

2 Working with 1 wonton wrapper at a time, place 1 heaped teaspoon of the Filling in the center of the skin and gather the sides of the wrapper around the Filling, forming natural pleats. As you work, press on the Filling to pack it tightly.

3 Tap each dumpling lightly to flatten the bottom and make it stand upright. Place the dumplings in a steamer basket over boiling water, cover and steam over high heat for 5 minutes. Brush the tops with the Garlic Oil. Remove from the heat to a serving platter. To eat, dip the dumpling in the Sweet-sour Chili Dip and finely sliced ginger.

Wonton wrappers are made from wheat dough, and come in a variety of sizes and thicknesses. They are filled with meat or vegetables, then steamed, fried or used in soups. Fresh or frozen wonton wrappers are available in most supermarkets.

Makes 30 dumplings
Preparation time: 30 mins
Cooking time: 5 mins

Place 1 heaped teaspoon of the Filling in the center of each wonton wrapper.

Gather the sides of the wrapper around the Filling, forming natural pleats.

Vietnamese Pork and Crab Imperial Rolls

Everyone loves these crispy Vietnamese spring rolls known as *cha gio* (pronounced "*cha yoh*"). These take a little time to prepare, but are well worth the effort.

12 dried rice paper wrappers (see note), each about 8 in/20 cm in diameter
Oil for deep-frying
1 portion Vietnamese Fish Sauce Dip (page 10)

Filling
2 oz (50 g) dried bean thread noodles, soaked in water for 20 minutes, drained, and cut into lengths (see note)
1 egg, beaten
8 oz (250 g) ground pork
1 cup (4 oz/120 g) cooked crabmeat
1 small onion, diced
2 green onions (scallions), minced
1 small carrot, grated to yield 1 cup (2 oz/50 g)
2 cups (4 oz/100 g) bean sprouts, tails removed, blanched and drained
$1/2$ teaspoon salt
1 tablespoon fish sauce
$1/2$ teaspoon freshly ground black pepper

Accompaniments
12 pieces butter lettuce leaves
Sprigs of mint leaves
Sprigs of fresh coriander leaves (cilantro)
1 small cucumber, cut into matchsticks

1 Make the Filling by combining all the ingredients in a large bowl and mixing until well blended.

2 To make a roll, briefly dip a rice paper wrapper in a bowl of water until soft. Remove and place on a dry surface, smoothing it with your fingers. Place 2 heaping tablespoons of the Filling along one side of the wrapper. Fold the closest edge of the wrapper over the Filling, then fold in the sides and roll up tightly, pressing to seal. Repeat until all the ingredients are used up.

3 Heat the oil in a wok or saucepan over medium-heat until hot. Gently lower the rolls into the oil, a few at a time, and deep-fry for 3 to 5 minutes each, until golden brown and crispy on all sides. Remove and drain on paper towels.

4 Place the deep-fried rolls on a serving platter with the Accompaniments and serve with dipping bowls of the Vietnamese Fish Sauce Dip on the side.

Bean thread noodles, also known as "cellophane" or "glass" noodles, are thin, clear strands made from mung bean starch and water. Soak in hot water for 15 minutes to soften. Available from Asian food stores.

Vietnamese rice paper wrappers are sold dried in plastic packets of 10 or 20. Other types of spring roll or wonton wrappers may substitute for rice paper wrappers although most of them are made from wheat flour and eggs, and the taste is therefore quite different.

Serves 4–6
Preparation time: **45 mins**
Cooking time: **20 mins**

Fold the bottom edge over the Filling, then fold in the sides.

Roll the spring roll away from you, keeping the edges folded in, until the paper is finished.

Chicken and Shrimp Morsels in an Egg Net

2 eggs
2 tablespoons minced
fresh coriander leaves
(cilantro)
1 to 2 bird's-eye chilies,
thinly sliced
2 tablespoons oil

Filling
2 tablespoons oil
2 cloves garlic, minced
1 teaspoon crushed fresh
coriander (cilantro)
roots and stems
1 teaspoon freshly
ground black pepper
8 oz (250 g) fresh shrimp,
peeled, deveined and
minced
8 oz (250 g) ground
chicken
1 teaspoon salt
2 tablespoons shaved palm
sugar or dark brown sugar
2 shallots, minced
4 tablespoons ground
roasted peanuts

1 To make the Filling, heat the oil in a wok over medium heat and stir-fry the garlic, coriander roots and black pepper for 1 to 2 minutes until fragrant. Add the shrimp and chicken and stir-fry until barely cooked, 2 to 3 minutes. Add the salt, palm sugar, shallots and peanuts. Stir-fry for another minute. Remove and set aside.

2 Beat the eggs in a bowl. Make a cone from a piece of banana leaf or waxed paper (or use a frosting cone). Pour a small amount of the beaten eggs into the cone. Lightly grease a crêpe or omelet pan with a bit of oil and heat over medium heat. Once the pan is hot, squeeze lines of the beaten eggs slowly onto the pan in a zig-zag pattern, shaping it into a 4-in (10-cm) square net. Once the egg has set, carefully remove from the pan with a spatula and set aside to cool.

3 When cool enough to handle, place a small amount of coriander leaves and chilies in the center of each egg net. Then place 2 teaspoons of the Filling on top and fold the sides toward the center. Fold in the remaining sides to make a small square package. Serve immediately.

4 A simple alternative to the egg net is to prepare a very thin omelet. Cut the omelet into the required number of squares, place the coriander leaves, chilies and Filling onto each square and fold to make a small package.

Serves 4
Preparation time: 30 mins
Cooking time: 30 mins

Make a cone from a piece of banana leaf or waxed paper (or use a frosting cone).

Stir-fry the Filling ingredients in a wok.

Squeeze lines of the beaten eggs in a zig-zag pattern to form a 4-in (10-cm) square net.

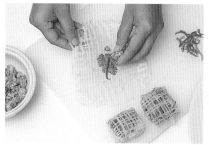

Fold the egg net over the Filling to make a small package.

Golden Dumplings

3 fresh coriander (cilantro) roots
5 cloves garlic, minced
5 black peppercorns
8 oz (250 g) fresh shrimp, finely chopped
8 oz (250 g) ground pork
4 oz (120 g) dried bean thread noodles, soaked in
    water for 20 minutes, drained, and cut into lengths
    (see note)
6 water chestnuts, peeled and finely chopped
$1/2$ teaspoon salt
$1/2$ tablespoon fish sauce
3 cups (750 ml) plus 2 tablespoons oil
30 small spring roll wrappers
30 green onion (scallion) leaves, blanched
Spicy-sweet Thai Dip (page 11)

1 Grind the coriander roots, garlic and peppercorns until fine. Transfer half of the paste to a mixing bowl. Add the shrimp, pork, noodles, water chestnuts, salt and fish sauce and stir well to combine.
2 Heat 2 tablespoons of oil in a wok or skillet over medium–high heat. Add the remaining garlic paste and stir-fry until golden. Add the shrimp and pork mixture and stir-fry for 4 or 5 minutes. Remove from the heat.
3 Place a spring roll wrapper on a flat surface and spoon 1 tablespoon of the mixture onto the center of the wrapper. Gather the edges together to form a small sack. Tie the sack with a green onion leaf and set aside. Repeat with the remaining wrappers.
4 Heat the 3 cups of oil in a wok over medium heat and gently put the sacks in the oil, a few at a time. Fry the sacks until golden brown. Remove with a slotted spoon. Drain on a wire rack. Serve with the Spicy-sweet Thai Dip.

Bean thread noodles, also known as "cellophane" or "glass" noodles, are thin, clear strands made from mung bean starch and water. Soak in hot water for 15 minutes to soften. Available from Asian food stores.

Serves 4 to 6
Preparation time: **20 mins**   Cooking time: **15 mins**

Spicy Balinese Chicken Parcels

1 1/2 lbs (700 g) chicken breast, sliced into strips
2 teaspoons tamarind pulp soaked in 2 table-spoons warm water, mashed and strained to obtain the juice
2 tablespoons plus 2 teaspoons oil
2 tablespoons minced shallots
1 tablespoon minced garlic
1–2 red finger-length chilies, thinly sliced
1/2 cup (125 ml) thick coconut milk
1/2 teaspoon salt

6–8 *salam* leaves or 3 sprigs lemon basil
3 banana leaf sheets, each about 10 x 18 in (25 x 45 cm), softened in hot water for wrap-ping (page 40)

Seasoning Paste
1 tablespoon coriander seeds
1 teaspoon black peppercorns
4 candlenuts
1–2 red finger-length chilies
4 shallots, peeled

3 cloves garlic, peeled
1 stalk lemongrass, tender inner part of bottom third only, sliced
1 teaspoon ground turmeric
1 in (2 1/2 cm) fresh galangal or ginger root, peeled and sliced
1 1/2 teaspoons palm sugar
1 teaspoon salt

Serves 4
Preparation time: **40 mins**
Cooking time: **45 mins**

1 To prepare the Seasoning Paste, dry-fry the coriander seeds, peppercorns and candlenuts in a skillet over low heat for 2–3 minutes until fragrant. Remove from the skillet and grind to a powder in a spice grinder. Add all the other Seasoning Paste ingredients. Process until finely ground, adding a little oil if needed to keep the mixture turning.
2 Heat 2 tablespoons of the oil in a wok. Add the Seasoning Paste and stir-fry over medium heat until fragrant, about 5 minutes. Transfer to a plate and set aside to cool.
3 Heat 2 teaspoons of the oil in the same wok. Stir-fry the shallots and garlic until translucent, about 2 minutes. Place in a large bowl and stir in the chicken, chilies, coconut milk, salt, *salam* leaves, tamarind juice and cooled Seasoning Paste, mixing thoroughly.
4 Wrap and cook the packages according to the steps outlined on pages 40–41. If banana leaves are not available, dish the filling into an ovenproof baking dish, cover and steam for 15 to 20 minutes.

Candlenuts are waxy, cream-colored nuts similar in size to macadamia nuts, which make a good substitute. They are never eaten raw but are ground and cooked with other seasonings. Store candlenuts in a cool, dry place.

Salam leaves are subtly flavored and comes from a tree in the cassia family. The taste bears no resemblance whatsoever to the taste of a bay leaf, which is sometimes sug-gested as a substitute. If you cannot obtain dried salam leaf, omit altogether.

Double-wrapped Banana Leaf Packets (*Tum*)

The banana leaf is a versatile cooking material that is widely used in preparing Asian dishes. It is frequently used to wrap foods for grilling, steaming, or grilling directly over hot coals. Almost any type of meat, such as duck, chicken, beef and even fish or eel, can be chopped, seasoned and wrapped in banana leaves to be cooked. To use, first rinse and wipe the banana leaf clean and cut it to the required sizes. Scald it with boiling water or heat it directly over a gas flame until it softens enough to be pliable without cracking. Fresh banana leaves are sometimes sold in Hispanic or Asian markets, but frozen banana leaves are more readily available. If banana leaves are not available, aluminum foil can be used, though it does not impart the subtle flavors that banana leaves do.

3 large sheets of banana leaf (about 10 in x 18 in/25 cm x 45 cm) as main wrappers
Small strips of banana leaf for outer wrapping
1 quantity Spicy Balinese Chicken filling (page 38)
Wok with cover and steaming rack or steamer set

  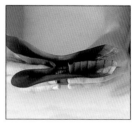

Step 1: Cut the large banana leaf wrappers into 8 x 9 in (20 x 22 cm) sheets. Cut the smaller strips 2 x 8 in (5 x 20 cm) for the outer wrappers. Place 2 tablespoons of the Filling in the center of a large banana leaf wrapper.

Step 2: Pleat one side of the wrapper with your index finger and press the two resulting folds of the leaf together as shown to form "wings".

Step 3: Repeat on the other side of the wrapper.

Step 4: Fold one wing from each side on the left and right to the front of the package.

Step 5: Fold the wings on the reverse side to the back of the package.

Step 6: Place the package in the center of a smaller strip of banana leaf and wrap it up around the pleats.

Step 7: Secure the top of both leaves with a single toothpick or staple the top with a stapler.

Step 8: Tuck in any open corners before steaming. Fill a wok or steamer with about 2 in (5 cm) of water. Bring the water to a boil. Place the packages on the steamer rack set inside the wok or steamer. Cover the wok or steamer and cook for 35 minutes, adding more boiling water as needed.

Spicy Indonesian Minced Beef Packets

1 lb (500 g) ground beef
3 eggs, lightly beaten
5–6 sour carambola, sliced (see note)
2–3 red finger-length chilies, deseeded and thinly sliced
8 *salam* leaves (optional)
1 cup (250 ml) coconut cream
4 banana leaf sheets, each about 10 x 18 in (25 x 45 cm), softened in hot water, cut into wrappers (page 40)

Spice Paste
3 teaspoons coriander seeds
$1/2$ teaspoon cumin seeds
1 teaspoon freshly ground black pepper
3 candlenuts or unsalted raw macadamia nuts, chopped
8 shallots, peeled
$1/2$ in (1 cm) galangal root, peeled and sliced
$1/2$ in (1 cm) fresh ginger root, peeled and sliced
4 cloves garlic, peeled
1 tablespoon palm sugar or brown sugar
1 teaspoon salt

1 Prepare the Spice Paste by dry-frying the coriander and cumin seeds in a pan or skillet over low heat until fragrant, about 2 to 3 minutes. Transfer to a spice grinder or blender and grind with the pepper and candlenuts until fine. Add the shallots, galangal, ginger, garlic, sugar and salt and grind until smooth, adding a little of the coconut cream if needed to keep the mixture turning.
2 Place the beef in a large bowl with the Spice Paste, eggs, carambola and sliced chilies. Mix thoroughly to distribute the seasonings evenly.
3 Place 2 to 3 tablespoons of the beef, $1/2$ *salam* leaf and 2 tablespoons of coconut cream in the center of a banana leaf wrapper. Repeat until all the remaining filling and wrappers are used. Wrap and steam the packets as described on pages 40–41.

Candlenuts are waxy, cream-colored nuts similar in size to macadamia nuts, which make a good substitute. They are never eaten raw but are ground and cooked with other seasonings. Store candlenuts in a cool, dry place.

Carambola is a pale-green acidic fruit about 2–3 in (5–8 cm) long that grows in clusters. Carambola is used whole or sliced to give a sour tang to soups, curries, fish dishes and sambals. Not to be confused with the larger, sweet, five-edged yellow-green starfruit of the same family. Sour grapefruit juice or tamarind juice are good substitutes. If using **sour carambola**, mix the slices with 2 teaspoons salt, let stand for 10 minutes to draw out some of the acidity, then rinse before adding to meat.

Salam leaves are subtly flavored and comes from a tree in the cassia family. The taste bears no resemblance whatsoever to the taste of a bay leaf, which is sometimes suggested as a substitute. If you cannot obtain dried salam leaf, omit altogether.

Serves 4 to 6
Preparation time: **35–40 mins**
Cooking time: **20 mins**

Malaysian Curry Puffs

The puffs can be made with many kinds of Filling, including potatoes, sweet potatoes and taro root. You may also substitute diced or ground beef for the chicken. If you prefer a vegetarian version of this dish, replace the meat with tofu.

8-oz (250-g) packet
  frozen puff pastry
3 cups (750 ml) oil, for
  deep-frying

Filling
1 lb (500 g) chicken
  breast, diced or ground
1 teaspoon salt
1 tablespoon soy sauce
5 fresh coriander
  (cilantro) roots
$1/2$ teaspoon white
  peppercorns
5 cloves garlic
2 tablespoons oil
2 teaspoons curry powder
3 tablespoons Worcester-
  shire sauce
1 teaspoon salt
1 cup (7 oz/200 g) diced
  onion
8 oz (250 g) boiled
  potatoes, diced

1 Defrost the puff pastry sheets at room temperature for 20 to 30 minutes, according to instructions on the label.
2 To make the Filling, combine the chicken with the salt and soy sauce and set aside.
3 Grind the coriander roots, peppercorns and garlic until smooth using a spice grinder or mortar and pestle. Heat the 2 tablespoons of oil in a skillet over medium heat until hot. Add the spice paste and stir-fry 2 to 3 minutes, until fragrant. Add the meat and continue to fry until the meat changes color. Add the curry powder, Worcestershire sauce and salt and stir well to combine.
4 Add the onion and potatoes and continue cooking until the mixture looks dry. Set aside to cool.
5 Roll out the dough and cut into circles of 4 in (10 cm) in diameter. Place 1 tablespoon of the Filling slightly off the center of each circle, fold each in half and pinch the edges shut.
5 Heat the 3 cups of oil in a wok or large skillet and fry the puffs until golden, or bake at 400°F (200°C) for 12 minutes.

Makes 24
Preparation time: **45 mins**
Cooking time: **15 mins**

Place 1 tablespoon of the Filling on the dough, slightly off-center.

After folding the circle in half, lightly pinch the edges to seal the puff.

Fried Tofu with Sweet and Sour Sauce

2 cakes (10 oz/300 g
  each) firm tofu, cut
  into 8 large cubes
  (see note)
1 cup (5 oz/150 g)
  all-purpose (plain) flour
1 teaspoon salt
1 teaspoon freshly
  ground black pepper
2 large eggs, lightly
  beaten
2 cups (4 oz/120 g)
  unseasoned bread-
  crumbs
2 cups (500 ml) oil
Sweet and Sour Apricot
  Sauce (page 9)

Serves 4
Preparation time: **40 mins**
Cooking time: **15 mins**

1 Wrap the tofu pieces in several layers of paper towels, applying light pressure to remove any excess water. Set aside on dry paper towels.

2 To prepare the tofu, mix the flour, salt and pepper in a small bowl. Dredge the tofu pieces in the flour mixture, then dip into the egg mixture and coat with the breadcrumbs.

3 Heat the oil in a wok over medium–high heat. Deep-fry several pieces of tofu at a time until golden brown. Remove from the oil with a slotted spoon. Drain on paper towels. Serve with the Sweet and Sour Apricot Sauce.

Tofu, or bean curd, is available in various textures ranging from silken to firm. **Firm tofu** holds its shape when cut or cooked and has a stronger, slightly sour taste. Tofu can be found in any well-stocked supermarket.

Crispy Shrimp Fritters

1 cup (5 oz/150 g) all-purpose (plain) flour
1 cup (5 oz/150 g) self-raising flour
1 1/2 teaspoons salt
1/4 teaspoon ground white pepper
1/4 teaspoon ground turmeric
1 1/2 cups (375 ml) or more water
7 oz (200 g) fresh medium shrimp, peeled, deveined
   and cut into short lengths
1 onion, peeled and sliced
3 garlic chives or green onions (scallions), cut into short
   lengths (see note)
1/4 cup (2 oz/50 g) fresh, canned or frozen corn kernels
   (optional)
Oil, for deep-frying

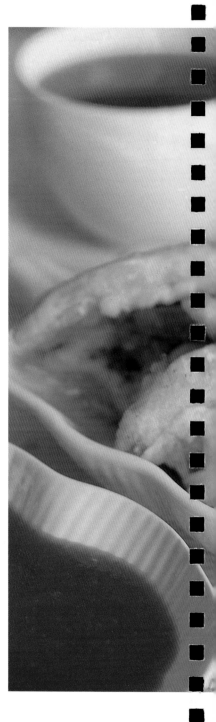

1 Sift both the flours together into a mixing bowl.
Add the salt, pepper, turmeric and water, and stir to
make a thick batter—it should fall off the spoon easily.
Do not beat the batter.
2 Add the shrimp, onion, chives or green onions and
corn kernels, if using, to the batter.
3 Heat the oil in a wok until very hot. Spoon heaped
tablespoons of the batter mixture gently into the hot
oil. Make sure that each tablespoon of batter has some
corn and shrimp in it. Deep-fry until golden brown,
about 4 minutes. Drain on paper towels and serve
warm with a chili sauce of your choice.

Garlic chives (*gu cai* or Chinese chives) have long, green
flattened leaves that resemble thin green onions. They
have a strong garlicky flavor and are often added to
noodle or stir-fried vegetable dishes during the final
stages of cooking.

Serves 4
Preparation time: **20 mins**
Cooking time: **20 mins**

Fragrant Thai Fish Cakes

1 lb (500 g) fresh or frozen white fish fillets
$^1/_4$ cup (60 ml) Red Curry Paste (page 10)
1 tablespoon fish sauce
$^1/_2$ teaspoon salt
1 teaspoon sugar
6 kaffir lime leaves, very thinly sliced
2 tablespoons tapioca flour or cornstarch
2 tablespoons all-purpose (plain) flour
1 egg
$^1/_2$ cup (4 oz/100 g) winged beans or green beans,
  very thinly sliced (see note)
3 cups (750 ml) oil
Cucumber Salad (page 10)

1 Process the fish in a food processor briefly until coarsely chopped, or slice and chop finely with a large knife. Combine the fish with the Red Curry Paste, fish sauce, salt, sugar, kaffir lime leaves, tapioca flour or cornstarch and all-purpose (plain) flour in a large mixing bowl. Stir well until the mixture becomes sticky. Add the egg, stir several times, then add the beans. Mix well.

2 Heat the oil in a wok over medium–high heat. Dip your hand in water to prevent sticking, then shape 1 heaped tablespoon mixture into a patty around 2 in (5 cm) across and $^1/_2$ in (1 cm) thick. Carefully put each cake into the hot oil and fry until golden brown. Remove from the oil with a slotted spoon. Drain on paper towels. Serve with the Cucumber Salad.

> **Winged beans** are an unusual-looking bean with four distinctive ridges running along their sides. They range in color from light to dark green. Top and tail as for normal beans. They may be eaten blanched or raw with relishes or added to salads, stir-fries or vegetable curries.

Serves 4 to 6
Preparation time: **20 mins**
Cooking time: **15 mins**

Thai Crab Cakes

1 cup (4 oz/120 g) cooked crabmeat, picked clean
$1/_2$ cup (4 oz/100 g) ground pork
1 medium potato, cooked and mashed
1 sprig fresh coriander leaves (cilantro), finely chopped
2 cloves garlic, minced
1 teaspoon fish sauce
1 egg, lightly beaten
$1/_2$ teaspoon salt
$1/_2$ teaspoon freshly ground black pepper
4 clean crab shells
2 cups (500 ml) oil

1 Combine the crabmeat, ground pork, potato, coriander leaves, garlic, fish sauce, egg, salt and pepper. Fill the crab shells with this mixture.
2 Steam the shells over high heat for 15 minutes.
3 Heat the oil in a wok over high heat. Fry the shells, meat side down, until brown. Serve with Sweet and Sour Apricot Sauce (page 9), if desired.

If crab shells are not available, form little crab cake patties and pan fry them over medium heat, 3–4 minutes on each side.

Serves 4
Preparation time: 15 mins
Cooking time: 25 mins

Shrimp in a Blanket

2 fresh coriander
(cilantro) roots
1 clove garlic
$^{1}/_{2}$ teaspoon salt
6 whole peppercorns
1 teaspoon soy sauce
12 fresh medium shrimp,
peeled and deveined,
with tails intact
6 spring roll wrappers,
cut in half
2 cups (500 ml) oil
1 cup (250 ml) Sweet
and Sour Apricot Sauce
(page 9)

1 Using a pestle and mortar or spice grinder, grind the coriander roots, garlic, salt and peppercorns until fine. Add the soy sauce. Marinate the shrimp in this mixture for a few minutes.

2 Wrap each shrimp in half a spring roll wrapper, covering the body of the shrimp but leaving the tail exposed.

3 Heat the oil in a saucepan or wok over medium heat. Deep-fry the shrimp, a few at a time, until golden brown. Remove the shrimp and drain on paper towels. Serve the shrimp with the Sweet and Sour Apricot Sauce.

Makes 12
Preparation time: **15 mins**
Cooking time: **10 mins**

Indian Spiced Potato Patties

2 slices bread
10 oz (300 g) potatoes, boiled, peeled and mashed
1 green finger-length chili, finely chopped
2 tablespoons finely chopped fresh coriander leaves (cilantro)
2 sprigs curry leaves
$1/4$ teaspoon ground turmeric
$1/2$ teaspoon ground red pepper
$1/2$ teaspoon salt
Oil for deep-frying

1 Dip the bread slices in water, then squeeze dry. Place the bread, potatoes, chili, coriander leaves, turmeric, ground red pepper and salt into a mixing bowl and mix thoroughly.

2 Divide the mixture into 10 balls and shape each ball into patties about $1^{1}/2$ in (4 cm) in diameter.

3 Heat the oil in a wok or saucepan and deep-fry the patties on both sides until golden brown. Remove and drain on paper towels. Serve with any of the various chutneys (pages 14–15).

Potato patties can also be grilled. Brush oil on both sides of the patties and grill over high heat for about 8 minutes until light brown on both sides.

Makes 10 patties
Preparation time: **15 mins**
Cooking time: **25 mins**

Tasty Cauliflower Fritters

1$^3/_4$ cups (180 g) channa flour
2 tablespoons rice flour
1 teaspoon salt
$^1/_2$ teaspoon ground red pepper
1 teaspoon cumin seeds, pounded coarsely or $^1/_2$ teaspoon ground cumin
$^1/_4$ teaspoon asafoetida
$^1/_2$ cup (125 ml) water
1 green finger-length chili, deseeded and finely chopped
1$^1/_2$ cups (10 oz/300 g) cauliflower, chopped
1 medium onion, grated
2 teaspoons ginger paste
Oil for deep-frying

1 Sift the flours, salt, ground red pepper, cumin and asafoetida into a mixing bowl. Make a well in the center and stir in the water to make a smooth thick batter. Add the chopped chili, cauliflower, onion and ginger paste to the batter and stir thoroughly.
2 Heat the oil in a wok or saucepan over medium–high heat until very hot. Drop tablespoons of the batter into the hot oil. Deep-fry until golden brown on all sides, about 1 minute. Remove and drain on paper towels. Serve hot with any of the various chutneys (pages 14–15).

Serves 4
Preparation time: 20 mins
Cooking time: 15 mins

Crunchy Corn Fritters

2 fresh coriander stems and roots
2 cloves garlic, peeled
$1/_2$ teaspoon whole peppercorns
8 oz (250 g) ground pork
2 cups (10 oz/300 g) fresh or frozen corn kernels or
   10-oz (300-g) can corn kernels, drained
1 large egg
1 tablespoon all-purpose (plain) flour
1 tablespoon tapioca flour or cornstarch (see note)
$1/_2$ tablespoon soy sauce
$1/_2$ tablespoon fish sauce
$1/_2$ teaspoon salt
2 kaffir lime leaves, thinly sliced crosswise (optional)
2 cups (500 ml) oil
Sweet and Sour Apricot Sauce (page 9)

1 Using a pestle and mortar, pound the coriander roots, garlic and peppercorns until fine. Transfer to a mixing bowl. Add the remaining ingredients, except the oil and stir well.
2 Heat the oil in a wok or large skillet over medium–high heat. Shape 1 heaping tablespoon of the mixture into a patty. Carefully slide each patty into the oil and cook on both sides until golden brown. Remove from the oil with a slotted spoon. Drain on paper towels. Repeat until the batter is used up. Serve hot with Sweet and Sour Apricot Sauce.

Tapioca flour is used as a thickener in doughs and pie fillings and sometimes in soups and stews as well. Tapioca flour does not become spongy when frozen and also imparts a chewier texture to baked goods.

Serves 4
Preparation time: **15 mins**
Cooking time: **15 mins**

In a mixing bowl, combine all the stuffing ingredients.

Divide the dough into 6 balls then, using thumb and fingers, form into a bowl.

Cauliflower-stuffed Indian Flatbreads

2 cups (8 oz/250 g)
  whole wheat (*atta*) flour
1/2 teaspoon salt
1 tablespoon butter or oil
3/4 cup (200 ml) plus
  2 tablespoons water
Oil or ghee for shallow
  frying

Filling
1 1/4 cups (8 oz/250 g)
  cauliflower, grated
2 teaspoons lemon juice
1/2 teaspoon salt
4 tablespoons finely
  chopped fresh coriander
  leaves (cilantro)
1 medium onion, finely
  chopped
1 green finger-length
  chili, finely sliced
1 teaspoon finely minced
  fresh ginger root

Makes 6 *paratha*
Preparation time: **45 mins**
Cooking time: **5 mins**

1 Sift the flour and salt into a large basin and rub in the butter with your fingertips. Bring the flour together with the water to make a soft, pliable dough. Knead until the dough is smooth and elastic, then cover and leave to rest for 30 minutes.

2 To make the Filling, put the grated cauliflower into a bowl and add enough hot water to cover. Cover and set aside for 5 minutes. Drain in a sieve, pressing with a spoon to extract as much liquid as possible.

3 In a mixing bowl, combine the cauliflower, lemon juice, salt, coriander leaves, onion, chili and ginger. Stir thoroughly and divide into 6 portions.

4 To assemble, knead the dough again and divide into 6 portions. Roll each portion into a ball, then using thumb and fingers, press the ball into a large bowl shape about 2 1/2 in (6 cm) across. Place a portion of the Filling into each dough bowl, then pinch the edges close. Try not to get the edges wet or they will be impossible to close. Shape into a ball again.

5 On a floured board, gently roll out the ball into a disc 5 in (13 cm) in diameter and 1/4 in (3/4 cm) thick.

6 Shallow fry the disc on a hot griddle until both sides are golden brown in color. Serve with any of the various chutneys (pages 14–15)

> **Atta flour** is a form of whole wheat flour. It is made from durum wheat that is ground very fine, with some of the bran included. Breads made from atta flour include chapati and roti.

Divide the cauliflower mixture between dough bowls, then pinch the edges close.

Place the paratha on a floured board and gently roll into discs.

Puffed Potato Breads

This light and delicious Indian bread puffs up when-fried, and tastes great served with various chutneys!

2 medium potatoes (10 oz/300 g)
1 1/3 cups (7 oz/200 g) flour
5 tablespoons plain yogurt
1 teaspoon salt
6 tablespoons water
Oil for deep-frying

1 Place the potatoes in a pan, cover with water, and bring to a boil, then simmer until cooked, about 10 to 15 minutes. When the potatoes are done, peel and mash until free of lumps. Set aside.
2 Sift the flour into a bowl and add the yogurt, salt and mashed potatoes.
3 Mix by hand to form a soft dough, adding sufficient water to soften. Knead for 10 minutes then set aside for 10 minutes.
4 Divide the mixture into 12 equal portions. Place a portion on a rolling board dusted with flour then roll it out into a pancake about 4 in (10 cm) in diameter.
5 Heat the oil in a wok until very hot and then deep-fry 1 or 2 puris at a time until golden brown.
6 Remove from the oil and drain on paper towels. Serve with Vegetarian Dal Curry (page 23) or with any of the various chutneys (pages 14–15).

Makes 12 pieces
Preparation time: **25 mins**
Cooking time: **20 mins**

Crispy Thai Rice Crackers with Dip

2 cups (500 ml) oil
10 to 12 puffed rice cakes
  (purchased, see note)
1 dried chili, soaked in
  water for 20 minutes
1 fresh coriander stem
  and root, minced
4 cloves garlic
1 teaspoon whole black
  peppercorns
1$\frac{1}{2}$ cups (375 ml)
  coconut milk
5 oz (150 g) lean
  ground pork
4 oz (100 g) fresh
  shrimp, chopped
$\frac{1}{2}$ cup (2$\frac{1}{2}$ oz/75 g)
  ground roasted peanuts
1 tablespoon tomato
  paste or ketchup
2 tablespoons palm
  sugar, shaved or
  crumbled
1 tablespoon fish sauce
$\frac{1}{2}$ teaspoon salt
2 tablespoons shallots,
  thinly sliced
1 sprig fresh coriander
  leaves (cilantro),
  roughly chopped
1 red finger-length chili,
  deseeded and thinly
  sliced

1 Heat the oil in a wok over medium heat. Fry the rice cakes, a few at a time, until lightly golden, turning to brown both sides. Remove and set aside on paper towels to drain.

2 Grind the chili, coriander root, garlic and peppercorns until fine, using a mortar and pestle or spice grinder.

3 Heat the coconut milk in a saucepan over medium heat until it begins to a boil. Add the spice mixture and stir a few times. Add the pork and shrimp and stir until well mixed. Add the peanuts and continue cooking for 5 minutes. Add the tomato paste, palm sugar, fish sauce and salt and continue to cook for 15 minutes more. The consistency should resemble chili con carne.

4 Remove the mixture from the heat and put into a serving bowl. Sprinkle with the shallots, coriander leaves and chili. Place the bowl on a platter and surround with the rice cakes. To serve, spoon the dip over each piece of cake.

Puffed rice cakes, made from puffed rice, is sold as a healthy snack food in North America and other Western countries. In North America, they are manufactured in several different flavors, and are becoming increasingly popular as a portable low-calorie snack. Puff rice is usually made by heating rice kernels under high pressure in the presence of steam.

Serves 6 to 8
Preparation time: 20 mins
Cooking time: 30 mins

Deep-fried Stuffed Crab Claws

10 to 12 fresh crab claws,
cracked and cleaned
1 cup (4 oz/120 g) fresh
or canned crabmeat
6 cloves garlic, minced
2 teaspoons crushed
fresh coriander
(cilantro) roots and
stems
2 teaspoons oyster sauce
2 tablespoons fish sauce
$1/_2$ teaspoon ground
white pepper
2 egg yolks
$2/_3$ cup ($1 1/_3$ oz/40 g)
breadcrumbs
Oil for deep-frying
Sweet and Sour Plum
Sauce (page 9)
1 to 2 limes, cut into
wedges, to serve

1 Crack the claws and carefully remove the meat reserving the claws and shells.
2 Mix the crabmeat, garlic, coriander roots, oyster sauce, fish sauce and pepper thoroughly. Add enough egg yolks to bind the mixture.
3 Grease your hands with oil and shape the crabmeat mixture around the claws.
4 Dredge the claws in the breadcrumbs to coat.
5 Heat the oil in a wok to medium hot. Gently lower the claws into the oil and fry until golden brown, about 7 minutes each. Remove and drain on paper towels.
6 Serve with the Sweet and Sour Plum Sauce and limes.

Serves 4
Preparation time: 20 mins
Cooking time: 10 to 15 mins

Add the egg yolks to bind the crabmeat mixture.

Shape the mixture around each claw.

Dredge the claws in the breadcrumbs.

Lower the claws gently into the oil and fry until golden brown.

Grilled Lemongrass Chicken Satays

Noodles and a green salad make fine partners for this delicious chicken, which you can serve as an appetiser or main course.

1 lb (500 g) boneless chicken thighs, cubed
12 bamboo skewers, soaked in water for 1 hour before using
1 portion Vietnamese Fish Sauce Dip (page 10)

Marinade
2 stalks lemongrass, tender inner part of bottom third only, sliced
3 shallots
1 red finger-length chili, deseeded and sliced
3 cloves garlic
1 tablespoon oil
1 tablespoon soy sauce
1 tablespoon oyster sauce
2 teaspoons fish sauce
1 tablespoon honey
1 teaspoon sugar
$1/4$ teaspoon salt
1 teaspoon sesame oil
$1/4$ teaspoon freshly ground black pepper

1 Make the Marinade first by grinding the lemongrass, shallots, chili, garlic and oil to a smooth paste in a blender. Add all the other ingredients and mix well.
2 Pour the Marinade over the chicken cubes and mix until well coated. Allow to marinate for at least 1 hour.
3 Thread the marinated chicken cubes onto the bamboo skewers and grill, a few at a time, on a pan grill or under a preheated broiler using medium heat for about 4 minutes on each side, until cooked.
4 Transfer to a serving platter and serve hot with the Vietnamese Fish Sauce Dip on the side.

Serves 4
Preparation time: 30 mins + 1 hour to marinate
Cooking time: 10 mins

Indonesian Chicken Satays with Peanut Dip

1 lb (500 g) chicken
  breast, cubed
24 bamboo skewers,
  soaked in water for
  1 hour before using

Marinade
2 teaspoons tamarind pulp
  soaked in 2 tablespoons
  warm water, mashed and
  strained to obtain the
  juice
3 cloves garlic, peeled
4 shallots, peeled
1 teaspoon coriander
  seeds
$1/4$ teaspoon cumin
  seeds
$1/2$ teaspoon salt
$1 1/2$ tablespoons oil

Peanut Sauce
2 teaspoons oil
2–3 bird's-eye chilies
3 red finger-length chilies
3 cloves garlic, minced
$1 1/3$ cups (7 oz/200 g)
  unsalted peanuts,
  dry-roasted and skinned
$1/2$ teaspoon salt
3 tablespoons palm sugar
  or brown sugar
1 cup (250 ml) hot water

Sweet Soy Dip
2 teaspoons oil
$1/3$ cup (90 ml) sweet
  Indonesian soy sauce
1 red finger-length chili,
  thinly sliced
1 teaspoon freshly-
  squeezed lime juice

1 To make the Marinade, grind the garlic, shallots, coriander seeds, cumin, salt and tamarind juice to a smooth paste in a blender. Transfer to a bowl and stir in the oil. Add the cubed chicken, mix well and set aside to marinate for at least 30 minutes.

2 To prepare the Peanut Sauce, heat the oil in a small saucepan. Fry the chilies and garlic over low to medium heat, stirring frequently until soft, about 5 minutes. Put into a food processor with the peanuts, salt and palm sugar or brown sugar, and process briefly so that the peanuts are still chunky. Add the hot water and process again briefly to make a thick sauce. Transfer to a serving bowl.

3 To prepare the Sweet Soy Dip, combine the ingredients in a bowl and set aside.

4 Thread 4 to 5 chicken cubes onto each skewer. Grill under a broiler or over a barbecue grill until golden brown on both sides and cooked, about 5 minutes. Serve with dipping bowls of the Peanut Sauce and Sweet Soy Dip.

If sweet Indonesian soy sauce is not available, you may mix 2 tablespoons dark brown sugar with 6 table-spoons of dark soy sauce.

Serves 4
Preparation time: 35–40 mins
Cooking time: 20 mins

Thai Pork Satays with Peanut Dip

1 tablespoon sweet black
soy sauce (see note)
1 lb (500 g) pork loin,
cut into cubes
24 bamboo skewers,
soaked in water for
1 hour before using
Coconut milk for basting
Cucumber Salad (page 10)

Makes 24 sticks
Preparation time: 30 mins
 + 2 hours soaking
Cooking time: 30 mins

Marinade
1 onion, coarsely chopped
3 cloves garlic, peeled
1 stalk lemongrass, tender
inner part of bottom
third only, sliced
3 slices fresh ginger
1 teaspoon ground
turmeric
2 teaspoon salt
2 teaspoons tamarind
pulp soaked in 2 table-
spoons warm water,
mashed and strained to
obtain the juice
1 tablespoon palm sugar
2 tablespoons oil
$1/3$ cup (90 ml) water, or
more as needed

Thai Peanut Sauce
2 tablespoons oil
2 tablespoons Red Curry
Paste (page 10)
$1/2$ cup (2 oz/50 g)
Crispy Fried Shallots
(page 13)
$1^1/_2$ cups (375 ml)
coconut milk
$1/2$ cup (3 oz/90 g)
roasted peanuts,
coarsely ground
2 tablespoons palm sugar
or dark brown sugar
1 teaspoon tamarind
pulp soaked in 1 table-
spoon warm water,
mashed and strained to
obtain the juice
1 teaspoon salt

1 Combine the Marinade ingredients in a blender and process until smooth. Pour the mixture into a large bowl.

2 Stir in the sweet black soy sauce and add the pork cubes. Marinate the meat for at least 2 hours.

3 To make the Thai Peanut Sauce, heat the oil in a wok over high heat. Add the Red Curry Paste and Crispy Fried Shallots and stir until fragrant, about 3 minutes. Add the remaining ingredients and stir well. Reduce the heat to low and cook until the mixture begins to thicken; thin with some water if it gets too thick. Remove from the heat and place in a serving dish.

4 Thread 3 to 4 pieces of meat onto each skewer. Cook over a charcoal fire or under a broiler until brown. Baste each side once with the coconut milk or oil while cooking. Serve with the Thai Peanut Sauce and Cucumber Salad.

Sweet black soy sauce is not widely available in the West but can be approximated by adding $1/2$ teaspoon brown sugar to 1 tablespoon of dark soy sauce. Hoisin sauce also makes a good substitute.

Spicy Indian Beef Kebabs

1 1/3 lbs (600 g) beef, cut into bite-sized cubes
2 tablespoons black cumin seeds (see note)
2 teaspoons *garam masala*
2 teaspoons ground red pepper
4 tablespoons plain yogurt
3 tablespoons garlic paste
3 tablespoons ginger paste
3 tablespoons grated raw papaya
3/4 cup (175 ml) malt vinegar
1 teaspoon salt
Oil or ghee for basting

1 Mix all the ingredients except the oil in a bowl and set aside for 4 hours to marinate.

2 Skewer the beef chunks 3/4 in (2 cm) apart and grill over charcoal or under an electric grill for 10 minutes.

3 Let stand at room temperature for 20 minutes and then baste with ghee and grill for another 5 minutes before serving.

Black cumin is called *shahjeera* in Hindi, and is not really cumin (nor is it *nigella*, for which it is frequently mistaken) but a unique spice which is shaped like sesame seeds and is 2 to 3 shades darker than normal cumin seeds. Substitute with caraway seeds if unavailable.

Serves 4
Preparation time: 20 mins + 4 hours standing time
Cooking time: 15 mins + 20 minutes standing time

Fragrant Sultana Lamb Patties

1 lb (500 g) ground lean lamb
$^1/_3$ cup (2 oz/60 g) raisins, chopped
1 tablespoon ground almonds or cashew nuts
3 tablespoons ginger paste
2 tablespoons garlic paste
1 teaspoon ground cardamom
1 teaspoon ground red pepper
3 tablespoons roasted channa flour
$^1/_2$ teaspoon mace (see note)
1 teaspoon salt
Oil for shallow frying

1 Combine all the ingredients except the oil in a large mixing bowl, mix well and set aside in the refrigerator for 30 minutes.

2 Divide the mixture into 10 roughly equal portions and roll into balls between the palms, then flatten into patties. Heat the oil in a pan and shallow fry the patties over low heat until both sides are light brown, about 10 minutes on each side. Remove and drain on paper towels.

Mace is the dried wrapping that covers the nutmeg seed. Its flavor is similar to nutmeg, but slightly more bitter. It is usually sold in ground form, but is sometimes available in whole blades. It can be substituted with nutmeg or cinnamon.

Makes 10 patties
Preparation time: **10 mins + 30 mins standing time**
Cooking time: **20 mins**

Chicken Tikka Kebabs

1$^{1}/_{3}$ lbs (600 g) chicken breast, cubed
Oil or ghee for basting
24 bamboo skewers, soaked in water for 1 hour
   before using

Marinade
4 tablespoons plain yogurt
3 tablespoons garlic paste
3 tablespoons ginger paste
4 tablespoons lemon juice
1 tablespoon channa flour
1 teaspoon ground cumin
$^{1}/_{2}$ teaspoon ground cardamom seeds
1 teaspoon ground red pepper
$^{1}/_{2}$ teaspoon ground turmeric
$^{1}/_{2}$ teaspoon *garam masala*
1 teaspoon salt

1 In a large mixing bowl, stir together all the ingredients
for the Marinade to form a smooth mixture. Add the
chicken cubes, mix well and leave to marinate for
3 to 5 hours in the refrigerator.
2 Skewer the chicken cubes and roast in a hot oven or
tandoor for 5 minutes. Baste with oil or ghee and roast
a further 5 minutes.

Serves 4
Preparation time: **10 mins + 3 hours standing time**
Cooking time: **20–25 mins**

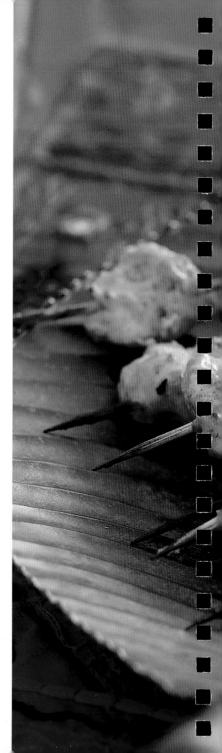

Caramel Glazed Chicken Wings

Vietnamese love the salty-sweet taste of food cooked in caramel sauce, and often use the sauce to enliven shrimp, fish, pork and chicken. These tasty wings will be the hit of any meal and are ideal partners for a mild-tasting vegetable dish.

2 lbs (1 kg) fresh chicken wings, cut into bite-sized pieces
1 teaspoon grated fresh ginger root
1 portion Vietnamese Caramel Sauce (page 12)

Place the chicken wings and grated ginger root in a large saucepan and pour the Caramel Sauce over the top. Bring the mixture to a boil over high heat. Reduce the heat to low, cover and simmer for about 30 minutes, stirring occasionally, until the chicken is cooked. Remove from the heat, drain off any fat and serve immediately.

Serves 4 to 6
Preparation time: 10 mins
Cooking time: 35 mins

Grilled Lemongrass Spareribs

2 lbs (1 kg) spareribs, cut into separate ribs

Marinade
2 stalks lemongrass, tender inner part of bottom third only, sliced
3 shallots
4 cloves garlic
1 finger-length red chili, deseeded
$1/2$ portion Vietnamese Caramel Sauce (page 12)

1 Prepare the Marinade first by grinding the lemongrass, shallots, garlic and chili to a smooth paste in a blender. Combine with the Vietnamese Caramel Sauce and mix well. Pour the Marinade over the ribs and rub it in with your fingers until the ribs are well coated. Allow to marinate for at least 1 hour.
2 Preheat the oven to 350°F (180°C). Bake the marinated ribs in the Marinade for about 20 minutes in the oven, turning over once, then turn on the broiler and grill the ribs for an additional 5 minutes on each side, basting with the Marinade, until well browned. Remove from the heat, transfer to a serving platter and serve immediately.

Serves 4 to 6
Preparation time: **15 mins + 1 hour to marinate**
Cooking time: **30 mins**

Grilled Vietnamese Meatballs with Peanut Sauce

These meatballs are equally good grilled over charcoal or broiled under an oven grill.

1 lb (500 g) lean pork or beef, sliced

2 cloves garlic, minced

1 tablespoon rice wine, sherry or sake (see note)

$1/2$ teaspoon sugar

$1/2$ teaspoon salt

1 tablespoon Roasted Rice Powder (page 13)

1 tablespoon fish sauce

1 tablespoon oil

12 bamboo skewers, soaked in water for 1 hour before using

1 portion Vietnamese Peanut Sauce (page 12)

Accompaniments

4 oz (120 g) dried rice vermicelli (*beehoon* or *mifen*), blanched for 1 to 2 minutes until soft, then rinsed with cold water and drained

1 to 2 heads butter lettuce, leaves washed and separated

1 cup (1$1/3$ oz/40 g) mint leaves

1 bunch fresh coriander leaves (cilantro)

1 medium cucumber, deseeded and cut into thin strips

$1/2$ small ripe pineapple, cubed to yield 2 cups

1 Make the meatballs first by combining the pork or beef, garlic, rice wine, sugar and salt in a large bowl, and mixing until well blended. Allow to marinate for at least 30 minutes.

2 Grind the marinated mixture in a food processor, then combine in a bowl with the Roasted Rice Powder, fish sauce and oil, and mix well. Wet your hands, spoon 1 heaping tablespoon of the meat mixture and shape it into a ball. Repeat until all the meat mixture is used up.

3 Thread the meatballs onto the bamboo skewers and grill, a few skewers at a time, on a pan grill or under a preheated broiler over medium heat for about 5 minutes each, turning frequently, until evenly browned and cooked through.

4 Arrange the meatballs with the Accompaniments on a serving platter and serve with bowls of Vietnamese Peanut Sauce on the side.

5 Invite your guests to wrap the meatballs in a lettuce leaf together with small amounts of all the other Accompaniments before eating it.

Rice wine is frequently used in Chinese cooking. Japanese sake, mirin or a dry sherry may be used as substitutes.

Makes 36 meatballs
Preparation time: 30 mins + 30 mins to marinate
Cooking time: 20 mins

Crispy Fried Chicken with Five Spice

This is one of the more renowned dishes from Sichuan, popular throughout China. It utilizes no fermented seasonings whatsoever, such as soy sauce or vinegar, relying entirely on the five flavors contained in the five spice powder. This permits the full flavor of the chicken to emerge, enhanced by the spices but not masked or altered by fermented products. For best results, and for optimum nutrition, it's best to use only free-range chickens.

12 chicken drumsticks
2 tablespoons five spice powder (see note)
1 cup (250 ml) oil
1 bunch fresh parsley, washed and drained
$2^1/_2$ tablespoons Sichuan Pepper-Salt powder (see note)
Chopped fresh coriander leaves (cilantro) and/or green onions (scallions), to garnish

Serves 4
Preparation time: 1 hour
Cooking time: 15 mins

1 Wash the drumsticks and pat dry with paper towels; dredge them in the five spice powder until evenly coated and set aside to marinate for 1 hour.
2 Heat the oil in a wok until hot, but not smoking. Add the marinated drumsticks to the hot oil and fry until golden brown, turning occasionally for even cooking, about 8 to 10 minutes depending on thickness of the drumsticks. Remove and set on a rack to drain.
3 In the remaining hot oil, fry the fresh parsley sprigs until crispy, about 1 minute; remove and drain.
4 Arrange the cooked parsley sprigs around the edge of a large serving dish, then place the fried drumsticks in the center. Sprinkle evenly with the Sichuan Pepper-Salt Powder, garnish with the coriander leaves and/or green onions, and serve.

Five spice powder is a highly aromatic blend of Sichuan pepper, cinnamon bark, clove, fennel and star anise, ground to a fine powder and used to season stir-fried noodles, in marinades and for sauces.

To make **Sichuan Pepper-Salt Powder**, dry-roast 2 tablespoons Sichuan peppercorns with $1/_2$ teaspoon salt in a dry pan, then grind to a fine powder.

Tandoori Chicken Fillets

4 large chicken breasts
(about 1$^1/_3$ lbs/600 g),
skin removed, 3 deep
cuts made on each side
1 green finger-length
chili, finely sliced
Ghee or oil for basting

Marinade
2 teaspoons ground red
pepper
2 tablespoons lemon juice
7 tablespoons heavy
cream
1 cup (250 ml) plain yogurt
3 tablespoons ginger
paste
3 tablespoons garlic paste
1 teaspoon ground cumin
2 teaspoons *garam
masala*
$^1/_2$ teaspoon salt
1 teaspoon freshly
ground black pepper
Pinch of saffron, crushed
(see note)
1 teaspoon ground
turmeric

1 Spoon the lemon juice over the chicken, sprinkle the
ground red pepper over them, and rub both into the
meat. Set aside.
2 Combine all the other Marinade ingredients in a
bowl and mix until smooth. Add the chicken and
work the Marinade into the chicken, making sure all
pieces are evenly coated. Marinate for 4–5 hours in
the refrigerator, or overnight.
3 Preheat the oven to 350°F (180°C).
4 Place the chicken on a roasting pan and cook in the
oven for 15 minutes. Baste with ghee or oil, turn the
chicken pieces over and roast the other side for
another 10 minutes or until the chicken is cooked.
5 Serve with slices of finely sliced green chilies.

Saffron is the world's most expensive spice. The dried
strands should be allowed to infuse in warm milk
before being added to rice and dessert dishes. Store
saffron in the freezer as it loses its fragrance quickly,
and never buy powdered saffron if you want the true
aroma of this spice.

Serves 4
Preparation time: **10 mins + 7 hours standing time**
Cooking time: **25 mins**

Grease your hands, wrap the Seasoned Shrimp around the middle of a sugar cane stick.

Grill the shrimp sticks until browned on all sides.

Grilled Vietnamese Shrimp Mousse on Sugar Cane Sticks

2 tablespoons oil
8 sugar cane sticks, each
  6 in/15 cm in length
1 portion Vietnamese
  Fish Sauce Dip (page 10)

Serves 4 to 6
Preparation time: 45 mins
Cooking time: 15 mins

Seasoned Shrimp
1 teaspoon salt
10 oz (300 g) fresh
  medium shrimp, peeled
  and deveined
$1/_4$ cup (2 oz/50 g)
  ground chicken
$1/_4$ cup ($2^1/_2$ oz/80 g)
  white fish fillet
3 cloves garlic
3 shallots
1 teaspoon sugar
1 egg white, beaten
1 tablespoon fish sauce
1 tablespoon Roasted
  Rice Powder (page 13)
$1/_4$ teaspoon freshly
  ground black pepper

Garnishes
1 head butter lettuce,
  leaves washed and
  separated
$2^1/_2$ oz (80 g) dried rice
  vermicelli (*beehoon* or
  mifen), blanched for 1
  to 2 minutes until soft,
  then rinsed with cold
  water and drained
  (optional)
2 tablespoons Crispy
  Fried Shallots (page 13)
Sprigs of fresh coriander
  leaves (cilantro)
Sprigs of mint leaves

1 Make the Seasoned Shrimp by rubbing the salt into the shrimp. Set the shrimp aside for 15 minutes, then rinse and drain. Grind the shrimp, chicken, fish fillet, garlic, shallots and sugar to a paste in a blender, then combine with all the other ingredients and mix until well blended. Divide the Seasoned Shrimp into 8 equal portions.

2 Lightly grease your hands with a little oil, wrap a portion of the Seasoned Shrimp tightly around the middle of a sugar cane stick. Repeat with the remaining ingredients to make a total of 8 sticks.

3 Grill the sugar cane skewers on a pan grill or under a preheated broiler using medium heat for 5 to 10 minutes, turning frequently until slightly browned on all sides. Remove from the heat and place on a serving platter.

4 On individual serving platters, arrange the cooked shrimp sticks on a bed of garnishes made up of lettuce, rice vermicelli (if using), Crispy Fried Shallots, coriander and mint leaves. Serve with dipping bowls of the Vietnamese Fish Sauce Dip on the side. The photo on the left shows an elegant presentation with sticks removed, however, half the fun of eating this dish is chewing on the sugar cane sticks.

Tender Fragrant Beef Noodle Soup

5 cups (1$^1/_4$ liters) water
1 lb (500 g) fresh rice
  stick noodles (*kway
  teow* or *hofun*) or 8 oz
  (250 g) dried rice stick
  noodles (*kway teow* or
  hofun), blanched for 2
  minutes in boiling water
  and drained
8 oz (250 g) fresh bean
  sprouts
1$^1/_2$ tablespoons Garlic
  Oil (page 13)
2 sprigs fresh coriander
  leaves (cilantro) roughly
  chopped
2 green onions (scal-
  lions), finely sliced
2 tablespoons Sweet-
  sour Chili Dip (page 13)

Stock
1 lb (500 g) oxtail or
  short ribs
1 lb (500 g) stewing beef
12 cups (3 liters) water
1 onion, cleaned but left
  unpeeled
1 tablespoon dark soy
  sauce
1$^1/_2$ tablespoons fish
  sauce
2 teaspoons salt
2 tablespoons soy sauce
10 cloves garlic, whole
1 small cinnamon stick
1 star anise (see note)
3 fresh coriander
  (cilantro) roots, crushed
$^1/_2$ Chinese celery root
$^1/_2$ teaspoon freshly

  ground black pepper
1 teaspoon sugar
1 in (2$^1/_2$ cm) galangal or
  ginger root, grated

Serves 4
Preparation time: **15 mins**
Cooking time: **2 hours**

1 Combine the Stock ingredients in a large stockpot and bring to a boil over
medium heat. Reduce the heat to low, cover and cook until the meat is very tender,
about 1$^1/_2$ hours. Add more water if necessary.
2 Meanwhile, in a large saucepan, heat 5 cups (1$^1/_4$ liters) of water over medium
heat. When the water boils, add the noodles, stir and cook 1 minute for fresh,
3 to 4 minutes for dried, or until tender. Drain in a colander.
3 To serve, put a portion of the noodles and bean sprouts into individual soup
bowls. Add 1 cup (250 ml) of the Stock and some meat to each bowl. Drizzle some
Garlic Oil on top and sprinkle with the coriander leaves and green onions. Serve
with the Sweet-sour Chili Dip or slices of red chili.

Star anise is a dark brown, strongly-flavored spice that resembles an eight-pointed
star. Its aroma is similar to anise or cinnamon. Store in a tightly-sealed jar in a cool,
dry place.

Malaysian Shrimp Noodle Soup

3 tablespoons oil
1 lb (500 g) fresh medium shrimp, peeled and deveined, reserve the heads and shells
5 cloves garlic, sliced
1 tablespoon sugar
8 cups (2 liters) water
2 chicken thighs or drumsticks
5 oz (150 g) dried rice vermicelli (*beehoon* or *mifen*), blanched for 2 minutes
8 oz (250 g) fresh yellow wheat noodles (*mee*) or fettucini
1 cup (2 oz/50 g) bean sprouts, blanched for 2 minutes
8 oz (250 g) water spinach, (see note), blanched for 1 minute
2 hard-boiled eggs, peeled and quartered
3 tablespoons Crispy Fried Shallots (page 13)

Chili Paste
12–15 dried chilies, cut into lengths, soaked to soften, deseeded and drained
2 red finger-length chilies
1 teaspoon dried shrimp paste (*belachan*), roasted
5 shallots, peeled
3–4 tablespoons oil
$1/4$ teaspoon salt
1 teaspoon sugar

1 Heat the oil in a wok over high heat and stir-fry the shrimp until they are pink, about 2 to 3 minutes. Remove from the oil and set aside.

2 Add the garlic and stir-fry until golden brown, about 1 minute. Add the reserved shrimp shells and heads, and stir-fry for 5 to 6 minutes until they change color. Add the sugar and stir-fry for another 2 minutes. Then add the water and bring to a boil. Reduce the heat to low and simmer for 30 to 40 minutes.

3 While the shrimp stock is simmering, prepare the Chili Paste. Grind the chilies, *belachan* and shallots in a blender, adding a little water if necessary to keep the blades turning. Heat the oil in a wok over low heat and stir-fry the Chili Paste until the oil separates from the mixture, about 5 to 7 minutes. Season with the salt and sugar, and transfer to a serving bowl.

4 Add the chicken to the shrimp stock and simmer for 20 minutes until the chicken is cooked. Remove from the heat. Drain the chicken and transfer to a plate and set aside to cool. Then skin, debone and shred the meat. Set aside. Reserve the shrimp broth.

5 Allow the broth to cool, then strain into a pan. There should be about 6 cups ($1^1/_2$ liters) of shrimp broth. Taste and adjust the seasonings by adding salt, pepper or a touch of sugar. Bring to a boil again before serving.

6 To serve, place a portion of the *beehoon*, *mee*, bean sprouts, water spinach, shrimp, chicken and eggs in a deep bowl. Ladle the hot broth over and sprinkle a generous spoonful of Crispy Fried Shallots. Serve immediately with the Chili Paste on the side.

Water spinach, also known as water convolvulus or morning glory, is a leafy green vegetable with crunchy, hollow stems. It is commonly used in Southeast Asian and Chinese cooking. It must be washed thoroughly to remove dirt and sand, and the thick, tough ends of stems removed. If unavailable, substitute normal spinach.

Serves 4
Preparation time: **40 mins**   Cooking time: **$1^1/_2$ hours**

Duck Noodle Soup

2 lbs (1 kg) dried rice stick noodles (*kway teow* or *hofun*), blanched for 2 minutes in boiling water and drained

2 tablespoons Garlic Oil (page 13)

1 lb (500 g) bean sprouts, tails removed and blanched for 1 minute

1/2 head leafy green lettuce, leaves separated and rinsed

3 green onions (scallions), thinly sliced

Freshly ground white pepper to taste

2 sprigs fresh coriander leaves (cilantro), chopped

1/4 cup (60 ml) Sweet-sour Chili Dip (page 13) to garnish

Crushed red chilies, to garnish (optional)

Stock

2 whole star anise (see note)

1 small cinnamon stick

1 duckling (about 3–4 lbs/ 1 1/2–2 kgs), cleaned

10 cups (2 1/2 liters) water

5 fresh coriander (cilantro) roots, crushed

1 in (2 1/2 cm) galangal or ginger, sliced

10 cloves garlic, crushed

1 teaspoon black peppercorns

2 tablespoons rock sugar

1/4 cup (60 ml) mushroom soy or dark soy sauce (see note)

1/4 cup (60 ml) fish sauce

1 tablespoon salt

1 To prepare the Stock, roast the star anise and the cinnamon stick in a dry skillet over medium heat until fragrant, 1 to 2 minutes. Combine the remaining Stock ingredients in a large stockpot and bring to a boil over medium heat. Reduce the heat to medium–low, cover and cook the duck until tender, but not falling apart, about 1 1/2 hours. Remove the duck and allow to cool. Strain the stock, discard the solids and return the stock to the pot. Skim any fat from the surface. Keep warm over low heat. Debone the duck and slice the meat into bite-sized pieces. Set aside.

2 To serve, place a portion of the noodles into individual soup bowls. Add 6 to 7 pieces duck meat, 1 teaspoon Garlic Oil, bean sprouts and several lettuce leaves. Garnish with the green onions, pepper and coriander leaves. Add 1 cup (250 ml) broth and serve with the Sweet-sour Chili Dip or crushed red chilies.

Mushroom soy sauce is soy sauce that has been infused with the flavor of straw mushrooms

Star anise is a dark brown, strongly-flavored spice that resembles an eight-pointed star. Its aroma is similar to anise or cinnamon. Store in a tightly-sealed jar in a cool, dry place.

Serves 6 to 8
Preparation time: 20 mins
Cooking time: 1 hour 40 mins

Chicken Noodle Soup

2 tablespoons fish sauce
8 oz (250 g) dried rice stick noodles (*kway teow* or *hofun*), blanched for 2 minutes in boiling water and drained
8 oz (250 g) fresh bean sprouts, tails removed
1 onion, thinly sliced
2 sprigs fresh coriander leaves (cilantro), roughly chopped
$^1/_2$ cup (1 oz/20 g) Thai basil leaves (optional)
1 lime or lemon, cut into wedges (optional)

Stock
One whole chicken, about 1–1$^1/_2$ kgs (2–3 lbs)
6 cups (1$^1/_2$ liters) Chicken Stock (page 12) or water
1 small cinnamon stick
2 green onions (scallions), cut in half
1 in (2$^1/_2$ cm) fresh ginger, grated
1 teaspoon salt
1 teaspoon sugar

1 To make the Stock, combine the ingredients in a large stockpot. Bring the mixture to a boil over medium heat, reduce the heat to low and cook for about 1 hour. When ready to serve, lift the chicken from the pot and leave to cool, then shred the meat. Stir the fish sauce into the Stock.
2 To serve, place some noodles in each soup bowl. Garnish with the shredded chicken, bean sprouts, onion slices, coriander leaves and basil. Add about 1 cup (250 ml) stock to each bowl. Serve each bowl with a wedge of lime to squeeze over the top.

Serves 4 to 6
Preparation time: **20 mins**
Cooking time: **1 hour**

Spicy Penang Tamarind Laksa

1 lb (500 g) mackerel or red snapper, cleaned
1 in (2^1/$_2$ cm) fresh ginger, peeled and grated
2 slices dried tamarind (*asam gelugor*)
1 teaspoon salt
6 cups (1^1/$_2$ liters) water
2 torch ginger buds (*bunga kantan*), quartered lengthwise (see note)
5 sprigs laksa leaves (*daun kesum*, see note)
2 teaspoons salt
3 tablespoons sugar
10 oz (300 g) dried laksa noodles or 1 lb (500 g) fresh laksa noodles

Spice Mix
15 dried chilies
2 teaspoons dried shrimp paste (*belachan*), roasted
2 stalks lemongrass, tender inner part of bottom third only, thinly sliced
4 red finger-length chilies, deseeded
8 shallots, peeled

Garnishes
1 small cucumber, cut into matchstick
1 cup (7 oz/200 g) fresh pineapple, cut into matchsticks
1 shallot, thinly sliced
1 torch ginger bud (*bunga kantan*), slivered
1 cup (1^1/$_3$ oz/40 g) mint leaves
1 red finger-length chili, thinly sliced

Serves 4
Preparation time: **40 mins**
Cooking time: **1 hour 45 mins**

1 Place the fish, ginger, tamarind slices and salt in a pan, cover with 1 liter (4 cups) water and bring to a boil. Reduce the heat to low, cover and poach the fish for 15 minutes. Remove from the heat. When the fish is cool enough to handle, remove from the poaching liquid, debone and set aside. Strain and reserve the fish stock; discard the solids.

2 To make the Spice Mix, first cut the dried chilies into lengths and soak in hot water for 10 minutes to soften. Then deseed and drain. Grind all the ingredients in a blender until smooth, adding a little water if necessary to keep the blades turning.

3 Place the Spice Mix in a large pan, add the reserved fish stock, the remaining 500 ml (2 cups) of water, the torch ginger buds, laksa leaves, salt and sugar, and bring to a boil. Reduce the heat to low and simmer for 30 minutes. Add the fish and cook for 15 minutes.

4 Bring a large pan of water to a boil and cook the dried laksa noodles for 5 to 7 minutes until tender. If using fresh laksa noodles, blanch in hot water for 1 to 2 minutes to revive. Drain the noodles in a colander and rinse under running water to remove excess starch. Drain well, then transfer to a serving dish.

5 To serve, place a portion of the noodles in individual serving bowls and ladle the fish broth over. Top with the cucumber, pineapple, shallot, torch ginger slices, mint leaves and chili. Serve with the Shrimp Paste Dip (page 11) on the side.

Torch ginger bud (*bunga kantan*) is the edible flower bud of the wild ginger plant. It imparts a subtle perfume to foods.

Laksa leaves is a intensely fragrant herb used in laksa dishes. There is no substitute for them.

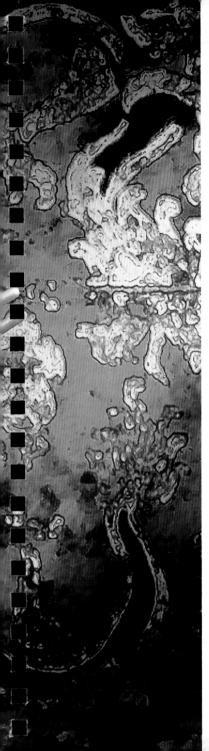

Thai Glass Noodle Soup

8 oz (250 g) lean ground pork
3 cloves garlic, minced
$1/_2$ teaspoon ground white pepper
1 teaspoon salt
$1/_4$ cup (60 ml) water
6 cups ($1^1/_2$ liters) Chicken Stock (page 12) or water
5 oz (150 g) dried bean thread noodles, soaked in water for 20 minutes, drained, and cut into lengths (see note)
4 dried black Chinese mushrooms or wood ear mushrooms, soaked in hot water for 20 minutes, drained stems removed and thinly sliced
1 cup (2 oz/60 g) chopped Chinese celery with young leaves
2 tablespoons fish sauce
1 teaspoon sugar
2 green onions (scallions), finely sliced
2 sprigs fresh coriander leaves (cilantro), chopped
Crispy Fried Garlic (page 13) for garnishing

1 In a mixing bowl, combine the pork, minced garlic, pepper and $1/_2$ teaspoon of the salt and mix well by hand, adding water as required.
2 Heat the Chicken Stock in a large saucepan over medium heat. When it boils, stir in the pork and return the stock to a boil. Simmer for 10 minutes.
3 Add the noodles, mushrooms and celery and season with the fish sauce, remaining salt and sugar.
4 Ladle the soup, pork and noodles into individual serving bowls and garnish with the green onions, coriander leaves and Crispy Fried Garlic.

Bean thread noodles, also known as "cellophane" or "glass" noodles, are thin, clear strands made from mung bean starch and water. Soak in hot water for 15 minutes to soften. Available from Asian food stores.

Serves 4 to 6
Preparation time: 30 mins + 30 mins soaking
Cooking time: 10 mins

Fresh Pineapple Shrimp Noodles

8 oz (250 g) fresh or dried wheat noodles or fettucini
$^1/_2$ cup (125 ml) coconut milk
8 oz (250 g) fresh medium shrimp, shelled and deveined
1 cup (10 oz/300 g) crushed pineapple, preferably fresh
1 green onion (scallion), thinly sliced

Dressing
$^1/_4$ cup (60 ml) freshly-squeezed lime or lemon juice
$^1/_4$ cup (60 ml) fish sauce
2 tablespoons sugar
3 cloves garlic, minced
2 tablespoons fresh ginger, grated

1 To make the Dressing, combine the lime or lemon juice, fish sauce, sugar, garlic and ginger in a mixing bowl and stir well. Set aside.

2 Cook the noodles in boiling water for 3 minutes. Drain in a colander and rinse the noodles under cold water.

3 Heat the coconut milk in a saucepan over medium heat and when it begins to simmer, add the shrimp and cook until just pink, about 3 minutes.

4 Arrange the noodles on a serving platter. Top with the shrimp and pineapple. Drizzle with the Dressing and garnish with the green onion before serving.

Serves 4
Preparation time: **15 mins**
Cooking time: **10 mins**

Grilled Lemongrass Beef Noodle Salad

This one-dish salad has the advantage of being both delectable and easy to make. You can prepare and assemble everything ahead of time, making this a perfect company meal. Partially freezing the beef firms it and makes for easier slicing. If you wish, you can substitute chicken breast for the beef.

1 lb (500 g) beef sirloin, flank steak or top round, sliced into thin strips

12 bamboo skewers, soaked in water for 1 hour before using

1 tablespoon oil, for brushing

7 oz (200 g) dried rice vermicelli (*beehoon* or *mifen*), blanched for 1 to 2 minutes until soft, then rinsed with cold water and drained

$1/2$ head leafy green lettuce, leaves washed and separated

1 medium cucumber, deseeded and cut into matchsticks

2 cups (4 oz/100 g) bean sprouts, tails removed

Sprigs of mint leaves

Sprigs of fresh coriander leaves (cilantro)

1 small carrot, cut into matchsticks

$1/2$ cup ($2^1/2$ oz/75 g) chopped roasted unsalted peanuts

1 portion Vietnamese Fish Sauce Dip (page 10)

Marinade

1 medium onion, sliced

3 cloves garlic

2 stalks lemongrass, tender inner part of bottom third only, sliced

1 teaspoon salt

$1/2$ teaspoon freshly ground black pepper

$1/2$ teaspoon curry powder (optional)

1 tablespoon fish sauce

1 Make the Marinade first by grinding the onion, garlic and lemongrass to a smooth paste in a blender. Add all the other ingredients and mix until well blended. Transfer the Marinade to a large bowl, place the beef in the Marinade and mix until well coated. Allow to marinate for 1 hour.

2 Thread the marinated beef strips onto the bamboo skewers and brush with a little oil, then grill on a pan grill or under a preheated broiler, basting with the Marinade, until just cooked, 2 to 3 minutes on each side.

3 To serve, place the rice vermicelli into individual serving bowls and top with the grilled beef, lettuce leaves, cucumber, bean sprouts, mint leaves, coriander leaves and carrot. Sprinkle with the peanuts and serve immediately, with a bowl of Vietnamese Fish Sauce Dip on the side.

Dress and toss this dish well with 2 tablespoons of the Vietnamese Fish Sauce Dip before eating it.

Serves 6
Preparation time: **45 mins + 1 hour to marinate**
Cooking time: **15 mins**

Fragrant Noodles with Chili and Sesame

1 teaspoon salt

8 oz (250 g) fresh or dried wheat noodles or fettucini

1 tablespoon sesame oil

2 baby cucumbers, deseeded and sliced thinly into long, thin strips

1 green bell pepper, deseeded and slivered

1 cup (2 oz/50 g) fresh mung bean sprouts, tails removed and blanched

1 small bamboo shoot, boiled and cut into fine strips (see note)

1 small onion, halved and thinly sliced

2 tablespoons black sesame seeds, toasted

Sauce

2 teaspoons red chili oil

2 tablespoons dark sesame paste or tahini blended with 2 tablespoons water

1 tablespoon sesame oil

2 teaspoons sugar

1 tablespoon black Chinese vinegar (see note)

1 teaspoon salt

1 In a large mixing bowl, stir all the Sauce ingredients together and blend until smooth. Set aside.

2 Bring a large pot of water with the salt to a boil and cook the noodles in the boiling water for 3 minutes.

3 Drain the noodles, rinse under cool water and drain again well. Place the noodles in a large bowl and drizzle with the sesame oil. Toss to coat evenly.

4 Add the vegetables to the Sauce in the mixing bowl and toss to mix well with the noodles. Place on a serving platter, or divide into individual portions in small bowls and sprinkle with the toasted black sesame seeds.

Bamboo shoots, are the fresh shoots of the bamboo plant. Pre-cooked bamboo shoots, packed in water, can be found in the refrigerated section of supermarkets. Canned bamboo shoots are also pre-cooked but should be boiled for 5 minutes to refresh before using.

Black Chinese vinegar is made from rice, wheat and millet or sorghum. The best black vinegars are well-aged and have a complex, smoky flavor similar to balsamic, which may be substituted. Chinese cooks add black vinegar sparingly to sauces, dips and when braising meats.

Serves 4
Preparation time: **25 mins**
Cooking time: **20 mins**

Noodles with Meat Sauce

8 oz (250 g) dried rice stick noodles (*kway teow* or *hofun*),
  blanched for 2 minutes in boiling water and drained
1 tablespoon sweet black soy sauce (see note)
1 teaspoon curry powder
2 tablespoons cornstarch
2 tablespoons fish sauce
8 oz (250 g) ground lean beef
4 tablespoons oil
4 cups (2$^1/_2$ oz/80 g) leafy green lettuce leaves, torn
3 cloves garlic, minced
1$^1/_2$ cups (375 ml) beef or Chicken Stock (page 12)
2 sprigs fresh coriander leaves (cilantro), chopped

1 Drain the noodles well, place in a bowl, separate them
and sprinkle with the sweet black soy sauce. Set aside.
2 Combine the curry powder, cornstarch and fish
sauce in a mixing bowl. Stir in the ground beef and
set aside.
3 Heat 3 tablespoons of the oil in a wok over medium
heat. Stir in the noodles and cook for 3 to 4 minutes,
or until heated through. Line a serving platter with
the lettuce leaves and place the noodles on top.
4 Add the remaining oil to the wok and stir-fry the garlic
until brown. Add the beef and stir-fry for 2 to 3 minutes.
Stir in the stock. Pour the meat mixture over the noodles
and garnish with the coriander leaves.

Sweet black soy sauce is not widely available in the
West but can be approximated by adding $^1/_2$ teaspoon
brown sugar to 1 tablespoon of dark soy sauce.
Hoisin sauce also makes a good substitute.

Serves 2
Preparation time: 15 mins
Cooking time: 10 mins

Bean Sprout Noodles

The sauce may be blended to suit anyone's personal taste and virtually any type of wheat noodle may be used. Moreover, sesame is a rich source of vegetable protein, minerals and other vital nutrients.

12–16 cups (3–4 liters) water
8 oz (250 g) dried wheat noodles or fettucini, or
  1 lb (500 g) fresh noodles
5 oz (150 g) fresh mung beansprouts, washed
  and drained

Sauce
3 tablespoons dark sesame paste or tahini
1 teaspoon salt
1 teaspoon sugar
1 tablespoon soy sauce
1 teaspoon vinegar
1 teaspoon freshly ground black pepper
2 green onions (scallions), minced

1 Bring the water to a rolling boil; do not add salt.
2 Add the noodles to the water and cook the dried noodles according to package directions, or about 30 seconds for fresh noodles. Test to make sure they are tender before removing from the pot.
3 Drain the noodles in a colander, rinse in cold water, drain and place in a large bowl.
4 Combine the Sauce ingredients in a bowl and add the Sauce to the noodles. Toss well to mix thoroughly.
5 Place portions into individual serving bowls, garnish with the beansprouts and serve.

For garnish, you may also use thinly shredded cucumber and carrot. For those who like it spicy, add 1 tablespoon of chili sauce or 1 teaspoon of ground red pepper to the Sauce, or sprinkle ground red pepper onto individual servings.

Serves 4
Preparation time: **15 mins**   Cooking time: **30 mins**

Tangy Tamarind Noodles with Shrimp

2 cups (500 ml) coconut milk

1/4 cup (60 ml) yellow bean paste or miso (see note)

2 shallots, sliced

1 tablespoon tomato paste or ketchup

5 oz (150 g) lean ground pork

1/4 cup (2 oz/50 g) sugar

2 tablespoons tamarind pulp soaked in 1/4 cup (60 ml) water, mashed and strained to obtain the juice

3 tablespoons fish sauce

13 oz (375 g) fresh shrimp, shelled and roughly chopped, to yield 1 cup (175 g)

1 lb (500 g) dried rice vermicelli (*beehoon* or *mifen*), soaked in water for 30 minutes and drained

8 oz (250 g) fresh bean sprouts, tails removed

1 cup (1 1/3 oz/40 g) snipped garlic chives (see note)

1 tablespoon oil

2 large eggs, lightly beaten (optional)

1 Heat the coconut milk in a wok over high heat. When it boils, add the yellow bean paste, shallots, tomato paste and ground pork. Stir well to combine. Reduce the heat to medium and cook until the mixture comes to a boil.

2 Stir in the sugar, tamarind juice and fish sauce, making sure to break up any clumps of meat, then add the shrimp and cook until they turn pink. Stir in the vermicelli, mix well and continue cooking until the sauce is absorbed, about 2–3 minutes. If the vermicelli do not soften completely, stir in some water and cook a little longer. Turn off the heat. Stir in the bean sprouts and garlic chives and mix them well. Remove to a serving platter.

3 Heat the oil in a skillet over medium–high heat. Stir in the eggs and cook through until firm without stirring. Slide the omelet from the pan and cut into thin shreds. Garnish the vermicelli with the egg shreds. Serve hot.

Garlic chives (*gu cai* or Chinese chives) have long, green flattened leaves that resemble thin green onions. They have a strong garlicky flavor and are often added to noodle or stir-fried vegetable dishes during the final stages of cooking.

Yellow bean paste is made from fermented yellow soybeans, and is an important seasoning in Asian dishes. Yellow bean paste (*miso*) is slightly sweet and is readily available at Asian food stores.

Serves 4 to 6
Preparation time: **10 mins**
Cooking time: **20 mins**

Thai Chicken Curry Noodles

2¹/₂ cups (625 ml)
coconut milk
1 lb (500 g) boneless
chicken, cut into bite-
sized pieces
2 tablespoons fish sauce
¹/₂ teaspoon salt
¹/₂ teaspoon sugar
2 cups (500 ml) oil
1 lb (500 g) fresh or
dried wheat noodles or
fettucini
1 green onion (scallion),
finely chopped
1 sprig fresh coriander
leaves (cilantro), chopped

1 large lime or lemon, cut
in wedges

Curry Paste
2 teaspoons coriander
seeds
¹/₂ teaspoon caraway
seeds (see note)
2 dried chilies
¹/₂ cup (4 oz/100 g)
onion, peeled and sliced
6 cloves garlic
5 thin slices fresh ginger
3 cardamom pods, seeds
only (see note)

¹/₂ teaspoon ground
nutmeg
¹/₄ teaspoon ground mace
3 whole cloves
2 teaspoons curry powder
¹/₂ teaspoon dried shrimp
paste (*belachan*)
¹/₄ cup (60 ml) water,
or more as needed

Serves 4
Preparation time: 20 mins
Cooking time: 25 mins

1 To make the Curry Paste, roast the coriander and caraway seeds in a dry skillet over medium heat until fragrant, about 2 minutes. Combine with all the remaining ingredients in a blender and process until smooth, adding water as needed.
2 Heat 1¹/₂ cups (375 ml) of the coconut milk over medium heat. When it comes to a boil, stir in the curry paste and cook until fragrant, about 5 minutes.
3 Add the chicken and stir well to mix. When the curry comes to a boil again, add the remaining coconut milk, fish sauce, salt and sugar. Cover, reduce the heat to low and cook until the chicken is tender, about 20 minutes.
4 Heat the oil in a large wok over medium heat. Fry about 5 oz (150 g) of the noodles until golden brown. Remove with a slotted spoon. Drain on paper towels and set aside for garnish.
5 Cook the remaining noodles in boiling water until tender, about 3 minutes. Drain and arrange the noodles in individual serving bowls.
6 To serve, pour the curry into a large tureen. Ladle the sauce over the top of each portion. Garnish each serving with the fried noodles, green onions and coriander leaves. Squeeze a wedge of lime over the top before eating.

Caraway seeds are small, crescent-shaped seeds used to flavor curries. They should first be dry roasted in a skillet over low–medium heat to bring out their aroma. Substitute with cumin or anise seeds

Cardamom is a highly aromatic pod containing tiny black seeds. If whole pods are used, they should be removed before serving. If seeds are called for, lightly smash the pods to remove the seeds. Ground cardamom is sold in packets or small tins.

Bean Threads with Shrimp in a Claypot

8 oz (250 g) dried bean thread noodles, soaked in water for 20 minutes, drained, and cut into lengths (see note)
8 oz (250 g) fresh medium shrimp, shelled and deveined
1 sprig fresh coriander leaves (cilantro), chopped, to garnish
4 cloves garlic, crushed
3 fresh coriander (cilantro) roots, crushed
1 in ($2^1/_2$ cm) fresh ginger, grated
1 teaspoon freshly ground black pepper
1 cup (250 ml) Chicken Stock (page 12) or water
2 tablespoons oil
1 tablespoon oyster sauce
1 tablespoon dark soy sauce

1 Line a claypot or casserole dish with the garlic, coriander roots, ginger and black pepper. Arrange the noodles on top. Put the shrimp on top of the noodles.
2 Pour the Chicken Stock, oil, oyster sauce and dark soy sauce over the shrimp and noodles. Cover and cook the mixture over high heat until the shrimp turn pink, about 5 minutes. Garnish with the coriander leaves and serve from the claypot or casserole dish.

Bean thread noodles, also known as "cellophane" or "glass" noodles, are thin, clear strands made from mung bean starch and water. Soak in hot water for 15 minutes to soften. Available from Asian food stores.

Serves 4
Preparation time: 10 mins
Cooking time: 5 mins

Rice Noodles with Beef and Vegetables

Leftover vegetables—and fresh ones, of course—complement the noodles in this meal-in-a-bowl.

3 cloves garlic, minced
$1/2$ teaspoon sugar
$1/2$ teaspoon salt
$1/4$ teaspoon freshly ground black pepper
8 oz (250 g) beef, thinly sliced
4 tablespoons oil
1 large onion, halved and sliced
4 green onions (scallions), cut into lengths
2 stalks Chinese celery, thinly sliced diagonally
1 carrot, cut into matchsticks
$1 1/4$ cups (4 oz/125 g) broccoli or cauliflower florets
8 dried black Chinese mushrooms, soaked in warm water for 20 minutes, stems discarded and caps sliced
2 tablespoons soy sauce
2 tablespoons fish sauce
$1 1/2$ cups (375 ml) Chicken Stock (page 12) or water
2 tablespoons oyster sauce
12 oz (350 g) dried rice vermicelli (*beehoon* or *mifen*), soaked in water until soft, then drained
Sprigs of fresh coriander leaves (cilantro), to garnish

1 Combine the minced garlic, sugar, salt and pepper in a bowl and mix well. Place the beef slices in the mixture and mix until well coated. Set aside for at least 15 minutes.

2 Heat 2 tablespoons of the oil in a wok over high heat. Stir-fry the marinated beef until cooked, 2 to 3 minutes and remove from the heat. Set aside.

3 Heat the remaining oil in a wok over high heat until hot. Add all the vegetables and stir-fry for 2 to 3 minutes until tender. Season with the soy sauce, fish sauce, Chicken Stock and oyster sauce and bring the mixture to a boil. Reduce the heat to medium, stir in the noodles, mixing and tossing until all the sauce is absorbed and the noodles look dry, about 3 minutes. Return the beef to the wok and stir-fry the noodles for 2 more minutes. Remove from the heat and transfer to a serving platter.

4 Garnish the noodles with the coriander leaves and serve immediately.

Serves 4 to 6
Preparation time: 20 mins
Cooking time: 10 mins

Classic Pad Thai Noodles

4 tablespoons oil

2 tablespoons garlic, minced

3 tablespoons dried shrimp

1 tablespoon preserved salted radish, chopped (see note)

8 oz (250 g) pork loin, thinly sliced

8 oz (250 g) fresh small shrimp, cleaned and shelled

1 lb (500 g) dried rice stick noodles (*kway teow* or *hofun*), blanched for 2 mins in boiling water and drained

2 large eggs

$1/_2$ teaspoon ground chilies, or more to taste

$1/_2$ cup (1 oz/20 g) garlic chives, sliced (page 48)

2 tablespoons ground roasted peanuts

8 oz (250 g) bean sprouts, tails removed and rinsed

Freshly-squeezed lime juice, to taste

Sauce

3 tablespoons tamarind pulp soaked in 1 cup (250 ml) water, mashed and strained to obtain the juice

1 cup (250 g) palm sugar, shaved and crumbled

1 cup (250 ml) water

$1/_2$ cup (125 ml) fish sauce

1 To make the Sauce, mix all the ingredients in a saucepan and simmer until well mixed and syrupy, stirring occasionally.

2 Heat the oil in a wok over medium–high heat. Add the garlic and stir-fry until golden brown. Add the dried shrimp and salted radish and stir a few times. Add the pork and shrimp and stir until the shrimp change color. Remove the shrimp to prevent over cooking and set aside.

3 Add the noodles to the wok. They will stick together so stir quickly to separate them. Add $1/_2$ cup (125 ml) of the Sauce and keep stirring until everything is thoroughly mixed. Add more sauce as desired. The noodles should appear soft and moist. If they look hard, add a little more Sauce or water and stir again. Return the cooked shrimp to the wok.

4 Push the contents of the wok up around the sides to make room for the eggs. If the pan is very dry, add 1 tablespoon oil. Add the eggs and cover with the noodles. When the eggs are cooked, stir the noodles until everything is mixed—there should be cooked bits of egg white and yolk throughout the noodle mixture.

5 Mix in the chilies, garlic chives and half the bean sprouts. Remove to a platter. Sprinke with the ground peanuts and remaining raw bean sprouts and a few drops of fresh lime juice.

Preserved salted radish or chai poh is pickled Japanese radish or daikon. Often added to dishes for its crunchy texture and salty flavor, it is available at Asian markets.

This recipe calls for a dark and sweet tamarind-based sauce which gives the noodles their amber color. Don't take any shortcuts or omit any ingredients. If you plan to make this for company, cook the noodles ahead and add the bean sprouts and garlic chives when you reheat the noodles.

Serves 2
Preparation time: **15 mins**
Cooking time: **10 mins**

Quick Stir-fried Basil Rice Sticks with Shrimp

Fresh wide rice stick noodles are commonly sold at Asian markets, though dried rice stick noodles may also be used. These are best when freshly made, but older noodles can be freshened by plunging them into boiling water to soften.

4 tablespoons oil
8 oz (250 g) fresh shrimp, shelled and deveined
3 cloves garlic, minced
1 lb (500 g) fresh wide rice stick noodles or 10 oz/300 g
    dried rice stick noodles (*kway teow* or *hofun*),
    blanched for 2 minutes in boiling water and drained
1 tablespoon sweet black soy sauce (see note)
2 tablespoons fish sauce
1 tablespoon oyster sauce
20 Thai basil leaves
8 oz (250 g) bean sprouts, tails removed and rinsed
2 dried chilies, crushed (optional)

1 Heat 1 tablespoon of the oil in a large wok over medium heat and stir-fry the shrimp for 1 to 2 minutes, or until the shrimp turn pink. Remove the shrimp and set aside.
2 Add the remaining oil to the pan and increase the heat to high. Add the garlic and cook for 20 seconds, then add the noodles and stir-fry for 2 to 3 minutes. Stir in the sweet black soy sauce. Return the shrimp to the pan and stir in the fish sauce, oyster sauce, basil, bean sprouts and chilies. Place on a serving platter. Serve hot.

If **sweet black soy sauce** is not widely available, add $1/2$ teaspoon brown sugar to 1 tablespoon of dark soy sauce. Hoisin sauce also makes a good substitute.

Serves 4
Preparation time: **10 mins**
Cooking time: **10 mins**

Stir-fried Rice Sticks with Vegetables

3 tablespoons oil

3 cloves garlic, minced

8 oz (250 g) beef, pork or chicken, thinly sliced

8 oz (250 g) dried rice stick noodles (*kway teow* or *hofun*), blanched for 2 minutes in boiling water and drained

$^1/_2$ cup (125 ml) Chicken Stock (page 12) or water

3 cups (7 oz/200 g) cabbage, shredded

8 oz (250 g) bean sprouts, tails removed and cleaned

1$^1/_4$ cups (4 oz/125 g) broccoli, or *bok choy*, chopped

2 green onions (scallions), cut into lengths

$^1/_4$ cup (60 ml) Sweet-sour Chili Dip (page 13)

Sauce

1 tablespoon yellow bean paste (see note)

1 tablespoon fish sauce

1 tablespoon sweet black soy sauce (see note)

1 tablespoon oyster sauce

1 teaspoon sugar

1 To make the Sauce, combine the ingredients in a small bowl and set aside.

2 Heat the oil in a wok over medium–high heat. Stir-fry the garlic until light brown, 2 to 3 minutes. Add the meat and stir-fry until it cooks through, 2 to 3 minutes.

3 Add the noodles and the Sauce. Stir to mix well. Add the stock and all the vegetables. Stir-fry until the noodles are moist and soft, about 3 minutes.

4 Spoon the mixture onto a serving platter. Serve with the Sweet-sour Chili Dip, as desired.

Sweet black soy sauce is not widely available in the West but can be approximated by adding $^1/_2$ teaspoon brown sugar to 1 tablespoon of dark soy sauce. Hoisin sauce also makes a good substitute.

Yellow bean paste is made from fermented yellow soybeans, and is an important seasoning in Asian dishes. Yellow bean paste (*miso*) is slightly sweet and is readily available at Asian food stores.

Serves 4
Preparation time: **10 mins**
Cooking time: **10 mins**

Southern Thai Rice Noodles with Beef and Broccoli

2 shallots, chopped
2 dried chilies
$^1/_2$ cup (125 ml) coconut milk
$^1/_2$ cup (125 ml) water
1 lb (500 g) fresh wide rice stick noodles or 10 oz/300 g
    dried rice stick noodles (*kway teow* or *hofun*),
    blanched for 2 minutes in boiling water and drained
8 oz (250 g) beef, thinly sliced
1 lb (500 g) Chinese broccoli or Western broccoli, stems
    peeled and sliced
$^1/_4$ cup ($2^1/_2$ oz/75 g) tamarind pulp mixed with
    $^1/_4$ cup (50 ml) water, mashed and strained to obtain
    the juice
2 tablespoons sugar
2 tablespoons sweet black soy sauce (see note)
4 tablespoons fish sauce

1 Using a pestle and mortar or food processor, grind the shallots and chilies until smooth.
2 Heat the coconut milk and water in a large wok over medium heat until it comes to a boil. Add the shallot mixture and cook, stirring, for 2 to 3 minutes.
3 Add the noodles, beef, Chinese broccoli, tamarind juice, sugar, sweet black soy sauce and fish sauce and stir to combine. Remove to a serving platter. Serve hot.

If **sweet black soy sauce** is not widely available, add $^1/_2$ teaspoon brown sugar to 1 tablespoon of dark soy sauce. Hoisin sauce also makes a good substitute.

Serves 4
Preparation time: **10 mins**
Cooking time: **10 mins**

Cantonese Fried Noodles

1/2 cup (125 ml) oil
4 oz (100 g) dried rice vermicelli (*beehoon* or *mifen*), broken into small pieces
12 oz (350 g) fresh or dried rice stick noodles (*kway teow* or *hofun*), blanched for 2 minutes in boiling water and drained
2 tablespoons soy sauce
2 cloves garlic, sliced
3/4 in (2 cm) fresh ginger, peeled and sliced
1 small carrot, peeled and thinly sliced
8 oz (250 g) chicken breast, thinly sliced
5 oz (150 g) fresh squid, sliced into strips
Salt and pepper, to taste
8 oz (250 g) fresh medium shrimp, peeled and deveined
4 cups (7 oz/200 g) *choy sum* or *bok choy*, washed and sliced
6 dried black Chinese mushrooms, soaked in warm water for 20 minutes, stems discarded and caps sliced, or fresh mushrooms, stems discarded and caps sliced
4 cups (1 liter) Chicken Stock (page 12) or water

1 tablespoon oyster sauce
1 teaspoon sugar
2 tablespoons cornstarch mixed in 1/2 cup (125 ml) water
1 large egg, beaten

Seasoned Sliced Chilies
10–15 bird's-eye chilies, deseeded and thinly sliced, or 1–2 red finger-length chilies, sliced thinly and combined with 2 tablespoons soy sauce in a small bowl

1 Heat the oil in a wok over medium heat. Add a small handful of the *beehoon* and stir-fry for a few seconds until they puff up but are still pale. Remove immediately and place on a paper-lined colander to drain the oil. Repeat with the rest of the *beehoon* and set aside.
2 Drain all but 3 tablespoons of oil from the wok. Reheat the oil over high heat and stir-fry the *kway teow* for 3 to 4 minutes. Drizzle 1 tablespoon of the soy sauce and mix well. Set aside.
3 Heat 2 tablespoons of oil over medium heat in a large pan and stir-fry the garlic and ginger until golden brown, about 1 minute. Increase the heat to high, add the carrot, chicken and squid, and stir-fry briskly for 3 to 4 minutes. Season with salt and pepper. Add the shrimp, *choy sum* and mushrooms, and cook for another 3 minutes until the shrimp are cooked and the greens are slightly wilted.
4 Add the Chicken Stock, oyster sauce, sugar and the remaining soy sauce, and mix well. Add the cornstarch mixture and stir to thicken the sauce, about 2 minutes. Then drizzle the egg in and allow the mixture to bubble and cook for 2 to 3 minutes.
5 To serve, divide the *beehoon* and *kway teow* into 4 individual plates or bowls. Ladle a generous portion of gravy over the noodles and serve immediately with the Seasoned Sliced Chilies on the side.

Serves 4
Preparation time: **30 mins**
Cooking time: **20 mins**

Hainanese Fried Noodles

2 tablespoons oil
4 cloves garlic, sliced
4 oz (125 g) chicken breast, thinly sliced
4 oz (125 g) fresh medium shrimp, peeled and deveined
4 oz (125 g) fish cake or fish fillets or deep-fried tofu,
   thinly sliced
2 cups (4 oz/100 g) *choy sum* or *bok choy*, cut into
   short lengths
1 lb (500 g) fresh yellow wheat noodles (*mee*)
   or fettucini
3 tablespoons Crispy Fried Shallots (page 13)
2 red finger-length chilies or 4 bird's-eye chilies,
   deseeded and thinly sliced

Gravy
1 tablespoon soy sauce
$^1/_2$ tablespoon dark soy sauce
$^1/_2$ tablespoon oyster sauce
1 teaspoon sugar
$^1/_2$ teaspoon salt
$^1/_4$ teaspoon freshly ground white pepper
Scant 1 cup (200 ml) water

1 To make the Gravy, combine all the ingredients in a bowl and set aside.
2 Heat the oil in a wok over high heat and stir-fry the garlic until golden brown, about 30 seconds. Add the chicken and stir-fry for 1 minute, then add the shrimp and fish cake or tofu, and stir-fry for 3 minutes. Add the *choy sum* or *bok choy* and toss until wilted, about 2 minutes.
3 Add the Gravy and bring to a boil. Then add the noodles, reduce the heat to medium and cook for 3 to 5 minutes until the Gravy thickens. Transfer to a serving platter or 4 individual serving plates. Garnish with the Crispy Fried Shallots and serve immediately with the sliced chilies on the side.

Serves 4
Preparation time: **20 mins**
Cooking time: **20 mins**

Complete Recipe List